Second Edition

OUNSELLING
in a nutshell

DATE DUE

Windy Dryden

Second Edition

COUNSELLING
in a nutshell

Los Angeles | London | New Delhi
Singapore | Washington DC

© Windy Dryden 2011

First edition published 2006
This second edition published 2011

SAGE Publications Ltd
1 Oliver's Yard
55 City Road
London EC1Y 1SP

SAGE Publications Inc.
2455 Teller Road
Thousand Oaks, California 91320

SAGE Publications India Pvt Ltd
B 1/I 1 Mohan Cooperative Industrial Area
Mathura Road
New Delhi 110 044

SAGE Publications Asia-Pacific Pte Ltd
33 Pekin Street #02-01
Far East Square
Singapore 048763

Library of Congress Control Number: 2010927762

British Library Cataloguing in Publication data

A catalogue record for this book is available from
the British Library

ISBN 978-0-85702-114-4
ISBN 978-0-85702-115-1 (pbk)

Typeset by C&M Digitals (P) Ltd, Chennai, India
Printed by CPI Antony Rowe, Chippenham, Wiltshire
Printed on paper from sustainable resources

Contents

Preface

I decided to edit the 'Counselling in a Nutshell' series because I saw the need for short, accessible texts on the main counselling approaches for people at the very beginning of their counselling careers. Since most people beginning counsellor training are exposed to person-centred counselling, psychodynamic counselling or cognitive-behaviour therapy, the texts in this series cover these approaches.

However, I also wanted to write a text that was broadly relevant to the practice of counselling, but was not specifically allied to any one approach. This book draws heavily on what is known as 'working alliance theory' based on the work of Ed Bordin (1979). From this perspective, counselling can be looked at as comprising a number of important domains: bonds, goals, tasks and views. What happens between counsellors and clients in these domains has a crucial impact on the effectiveness of counselling no matter what approach to counselling is practised by the counsellors. As such, I see this volume as being a companion to the other volumes in the series. While counselling can and does occur in different arenas (i.e. individual counselling, group counselling, couple counselling and group counselling), I will focus exclusively on individual counselling in this book.

In this second edition, I have made the following changes:

- While I have retained the essence of the general focus of the first edition, I have endeavoured to be more even handed towards person-centred counselling and psychodynamic counselling in my coverage. To this end, I interviewed Roger Casemore (author of *Person-centred Counselling in a Nutshell*) and Susan Howard (author of *Psychodynamic Counselling in a Nutshell*) and have incorporated their views at salient points in the text. My thanks to them for their time and input.

- I have included greater discussion of the influence of the context in which counselling takes place on the work of counsellors.
- I have included five discussion issues at the end of each chapter that are designed to stimulate your thinking on the subject and to encourage exploration with your colleagues.

Windy Dryden
London and Eastbourne

ONE

The Components of Counselling in a Nutshell

Counselling is a word that is much used, but as an activity it is much misunderstood. If I am going to present counselling in a nutshell, it is important that I make quite clear what I think counselling is and important that you understand how I am using the term. I am not going to offer you a formal definition of counselling, although I will presently discuss the current definition of counselling offered by the British Association for Counselling and Psychotherapy (BACP). What I will do is to outline the main components of counselling. Since this book is devoted to presenting counselling in a nutshell as it pertains to working with individuals (as I mentioned in the Preface), the components that I will outline and discuss in this chapter should be read as applying to individual counselling. My task is made more difficult since I will be endeavouring to present ideas that are broadly acceptable to adherents of the three main counselling approaches – psychodynamic, person-centred and cognitive-behavioural – as well as to those who consider themselves to be eclectic or integrative practitioners (that is, those who do not consider themselves to be adherents of any one counselling approach, but who draw upon different approaches in their work).

Please bear in mind as I write that I am referring to the ideal. Sadly, as is well documented, counselling does not always have helpful outcomes for clients and, just as sadly, counsellors do not always act in the best interests of their clients.

The components of counselling

In this chapter I will briefly outline some of the most important components of counselling. Let us begin by looking at the person who is adopting the role of counsellor, namely, you.

The counsellor

When you adopt the role of counsellor, you bring to counselling a number of ingredients. I will briefly discuss these ingredients one at a time.

A communicated genuine desire to be helpful to clients

Without a genuine desire to help your clients, you will just be going through the motions and this will probably be sensed by clients. As such, this genuine desire to be helpful needs to be both communicated by you, as counsellor, and experienced by your clients. If you are a trainee and your major motivation for seeing clients is to practise your counselling skills, or to get the required 'hours' to fulfil your course requirements, then again you will probably communicate this at some level and it will be picked up by your clients with less than satisfactory results.

A demonstrated acceptance and respect for clients

Your attitude towards your clients will have a marked effect on your counselling work. If you accept and respect them and this is experienced by them, then this will encourage them to trust you and open up to you. However, if you demonstrate a negative attitude towards them by not accepting them or even disrespecting them, then counselling will, in all probability, stall.

An ability to listen to and understand clients' psychological pain from their perspective

While a genuine desire to help clients is a central building block for counselling, this desire will count for little if you are not able to listen to and understand what your clients have to say to you from their point of view. The ability to listen to clients is a fundamental quality. It involves creating an environment in which clients feel safe enough to disclose their personal pain to you. This is dependent upon your doing a number of things, including: keeping relatively quiet while clients talk, intervening only to encourage them to continue their exploration; demonstrating non-verbally a keen interest in what they are saying; and communicating a non-judgemental, accepting attitude.

While listening is a key quality, its therapeutic power is enhanced when it is used in the service of understanding your clients from their point of view. In *To Kill a Mockingbird* by Harper Lee (1960) Atticus Finch says: 'You never really understand a person until you consider things from his point of view – until you climb inside of his skin and walk around in it.' Fortunately, you will not be called upon to do this literally in counselling, but being a counsellor will require you to view the world through your client's eyes *as if* you were inside his or her skin and walking around in it. As we will see in Chapter 2, this 'as if' quality is important. Unless you understand your clients from their perspective you will not be able to convey this understanding to them and they will not feel understood, and when clients do not feel understood the success of counselling is severely compromised.

Excellent therapeutic communication skills

You may be able to understand what your clients say to you, but this ability will not count for much if you do not succeed in conveying this understanding to them. Communicating empathic understanding to clients is a crucial skill and one that is recognised by all forms of counselling. However, there are other important therapeutic communication skills, some of which are emphasised more in certain approaches than in others. For example, in psychodynamic counselling making interpretations is a key therapeutic communication skill, particularly with clients whose problems are rooted in past conflicts and who have developmental deficits (Howard, 2010). Where clients' problems are rooted in conflicts, the assumption is made that such clients have a sufficiently functioning ego and can thus be helped to understand the connection between their present and past feelings, thinking and behaviour and how these are linked to certain unresolved conflicts in their life or internal world.

However, when problems involve deficits, such clients are deemed not to have a functioning ego and thus the purpose of such interpretations is to help the person become aware of certain aspects of their experience that they do not find it easy to identify, such as feelings and thoughts (Howard, personal communication). This helps the ego development of such clients. Communicating all this needs to be done skilfully if clients are to make use of such understanding, and issues of timing, the amount of information given, and the language used are all important skill considerations. Because good therapeutic communication is a skill, being able to learn, practise and get feedback on these skills should be a central feature of counsellor training courses.

Training that is sufficient to help the clients you are asked to see

As a counsellor, you will need to be trained. You may have a very therapeutic personality and your heart may be in the right place, but you will still have to be trained to acquire the knowledge, skills and professional discipline required to put your talent and desire to be helpful to best use. I am often asked how much training a person needs to have to be a counsellor. If you are on a professional training course, then this will have been laid down for you by one of the professional training bodies that exist in Britain today. However, if you are not training professionally and you are counselling clients in the voluntary sector, then you will need to receive sufficient training to enable you to do the work effectively and safely.

Your personal strengths and weaknesses

When I was trained as a Samaritan many years ago, we were told to leave ourselves outside the door when we came on duty. This is not the case with counselling. The three major traditions in counselling all recognise that counselling is a personal encounter between counsellor and client, although each has a different idea about the nature of that personal encounter, as we shall soon see (Chapter 2). Given the fact that counselling is a personal encounter, albeit one where the focus is on the well-being of one of the participants, it is important to consider what you bring to the encounter as a person. Although you are in the role of counsellor, your behaviour in that role is influenced for better or worse by your own personal strengths and weaknesses. This is why most approaches to counselling require their practitioners to be involved in personal therapy or personal development work so that they can monitor the impact of their personal contribution to the counselling process.

The client

Your clients also bring to counselling a number of ingredients. I will briefly discuss these ingredients, again one at a time.

Personal pain

In most cases, your clients will be seeking counselling because they are in some degree of personal pain. This pain may be focused on and reactive to a given life adversity (such as a bereavement or being made redundant) or it may be enduring and more pervasive (for example, chronic low self-esteem). In a small number of cases, your clients will not be in pain, but rather they may be seeking counselling for some other reason, for example as a course requirement or out of interest. In my view, these are still legitimate reasons for seeking counselling and, in such cases, it often transpires that these people are in personal pain, but are not explicit about this at the outset.

In the 1960s and 1970s (a decade when I began my career as a counsellor), counselling was more likely to be sought by people who were not in personal pain, but who wanted to develop their personal potential. While this does not happen so much these days – indeed such people tend to seek life coaching – counselling for personal development rather than for personal pain is also a legitimate help-seeking reason.

It used to be widely held that counselling was a short-term intervention for people whose personal pain was focused and of short duration, while psychotherapy was longer-term and for people whose personal pain was more pervasive and chronic. However, a number of factors led to the blurring of these boundaries. First, people in the field struggled to differentiate counselling and psychotherapy as activities. In other words, it was not clear that the ways in which counsellors worked was reliably different from the ways in which psychotherapists worked. Secondly, people who deem themselves to be counsellors see people with pervasive and chronic problems, while those who deem themselves to be psychotherapists see people with focused and shorter-lasting problems. Thirdly, counselling can be long-term and psychotherapy can be short-term. In recognition of some of these factors, and in response to their membership, the British Association for Counselling in September 2000 became the British Association for Counselling and Psychotherapy.

Help-seeking by choice

Counselling is based on the idea that your clients have chosen to seek help. Now, it may be that some of your clients have been mandated by the courts to 'attend' counselling, meaning that they can choose either to go for counselling or be sent to prison. While this is not the same as freely seeking counselling help, your 'mandated' client has still exercised a choice in that he (in this case) has chosen to see you instead of being sent to prison. He may show much greater resistance to being in counselling than a client who has chosen to see you without constraint, but he has still exercised a choice.

Clients' personal issues may well affect their behaviour in counselling

As I mentioned above, clients come to counselling in the main because they are in some kind of personal pain. While their personal problems relate to their life outside counselling, they may well bring these problems to counselling and thus these personal issues may well have a decided effect on their behaviour in counselling sessions. Indeed, there are some counsellors who hold the view that all client behaviours are a function of the issues with which they struggle outside counselling. Even if you don't agree with this viewpoint, it is important that you recognise that your clients' personal problems may well be played out with you since you may become a significant figure in their lives.

The working alliance between counsellor and client

At the end of the 1970s, Ed Bordin (1979) published a very important article which argued that counselling and psychotherapy could best be understood as an alliance between counsellor and client, both of whom have work to do in the process. He argued that the resultant 'working alliance' has three features.

The 'bond' between you and your clients

This component focuses on the interpersonal relationship between you and your clients. There are a number of factors that need to be considered when examining the bond components of the working alliance and I will discuss these factors in Chapter 2.

The 'goals' of the counselling

You and your clients come together for a purpose and this component focuses on this purpose and on the direction of counselling. In the late 1960s, Alvin Mahrer (1967) edited a book entitled *The Goals of Psychotherapy*. In his closing chapter, Mahrer argued that the goals that his contributors focused on could be split into two types: (1) amelioration of psychological distress and (2) promotion of psychological growth. I have already mentioned that over the years the focus of counselling has moved more from the latter to the former. However, both are legitimate goals of counselling and should be considered. I will discuss the issue of goals more extensively in Chapter 4.

The 'tasks' that both you and your clients have to carry out in order to achieve these goals

The tasks of counselling are activities that both you and your clients engage in that ideally are in the service of the clients' goals. While there are probably a number of tasks common to all counselling approaches (for example, the client disclosing her problems and/or life dissatisfaction), each approach has its unique tasks that counsellors and clients are called upon to engage in. I will discuss the task domain of counselling in Chapter 5.

To this list I have added a fourth feature known as 'views'.

The 'views' that both you and your client have about salient aspects of the client's problems and about the nature of counselling and the counselling process

Your attempts to understand your clients are likely to be influenced, at least in part, by the constructs put forward by the approach in which you have been or are being trained. This is also the case when we consider your attempts to help your clients. Different approaches to counselling emphasise different constructs and may use different language to describe similar constructs. The other books in this series will make clear which constructs are used by which approach when understanding and helping clients.

Your clients are also likely to come to counselling with some idea of what determines their problems and the nature of the help that you will be providing them. If we consider the latter issue, for example, these ideas may be well informed and accurate, as in the case of a person who has read about a particular counselling approach and has sought a practitioner of that approach because she (in this case) has resonated with it and has a clear idea of what to expect. On the other hand, this idea may be inaccurate, as in the case of a person who expects advice from a practitioner who is very unlikely to give it (for example, a person-centred counsellor).

As you will see, this book is largely based on this expanded view of the working alliance concept and I devote one chapter to each of the four components of the alliance.

Counselling is an ethical enterprise

A central component of counselling is its ethical dimension. While a full discussion of the ethics of the counselling relationship is outside the scope of this volume (see Bond, 2000, for a more comprehensive treatment of this subject), I do want to outline briefly a number of important ethical considerations.

The principle of 'informed consent'

It is a prime ethical feature of counselling that clients give their informed consent to proceed with counselling. This involves your informing their clients about salient aspects of counselling (e.g. how you, as counsellor, work and the practicalities of being in counselling with you, such as fees, the frequency of counselling sessions, and your cancellation policy) and clients giving their consent to proceed on the basis of such information. I will discuss this issue more fully in Chapter 3).

Confidentiality

One of the defining aspects of the counselling relationship is its confidential nature. This means that, with stated exceptions, clients can expect you to keep to yourself what you are told by your clients during counselling. This is summed up in the often quoted piece of advice given to counsellors: 'What you hear here, stays here.' A complete discussion of this complex topic is beyond the scope of this book although I will discuss it further in Chapter 4 (see Bond, 2000, for a fuller discussion of confidentiality in counselling).

Protection and development

Research has clearly shown that counselling and psychotherapy can have unhelpful as well as beneficial effects on clients (Lambert and Ogler, 2004). It is also recognised that counselling can be a stressful occupation and that doing such work can have harmful effects on you and your counsellor colleagues. Given these two points, it is another ethical feature of counselling that you engage in a number of activities designed to protect the welfare of your clients as well as your own. Three major activities fall under this heading.

1. Supervision

It is now a professional requirement for counsellors to have their work supervised. Supervision of your counselling work enables you to offer your clients a more effective and safer service. It is also designed to protect you. Counselling can be very stressful and sensitive supervision of your work can help to minimise this stress and enable you to avoid burn-out.

2. Personal therapy and/or personal development

In Britain it is a criterion for professional accreditation in the British Association for Counselling and Psychotherapy (BACP) and in most of the organisations that fall under the umbrella of the United Kingdom Council for Psychotherapy (UKCP) that practitioners have had to have engaged in personal therapy or some form of personal development. This is in recognition of the fact that counselling is personally demanding and that you need to understand both the impact that your work has on your own personal functioning and the impact that you may have as a person on your clients and on the counselling process. Different counselling approaches advocate different activities under the rubric of personal therapy/personal development and vary according to how much therapy/development is advocated.

3. Continuing professional development

It is now agreed by virtually all professional counselling organisations that some form of continuing professional development is necessary if counsellors are to have their accreditation renewed. My view is that you should engage in CPD activities both within your counselling approach (to keep abreast of new developments) and also outside it (to learn about and consider integrating the best that other approaches have to offer).

Counselling is a 'process'

The major goal of counselling may be said to help clients live more resourcefully, as free as possible from the restraining influence of emotional disturbance. How you and your clients go about working towards achieving this goal is going to be dependent in part upon your therapeutic orientation as counsellor. However, no matter which approach to counselling you use, the developing relationship between you and your clients can be viewed as a process from beginning to end. Indeed, one of the major features of the books in the *Counselling in Action* series that I edit for Sage Publications is that authors write about specific approaches to counselling as they unfold over time from the beginning phase through the middle phase to the ending phase. Specific issues become salient at each of the three phases and I discuss a sample of these issues in Chapter 6. For a more detailed examination of counselling as a process, see the second edition of *Key Issues for Counselling in Action* (Dryden and Reeves, 2008).

The context that frames counselling has an impact on its practice

While counselling is a confidential relationship between counsellor and client (with stated exceptions as mentioned above), it is not free from outside influence. Indeed, the context in which counselling occurs exerts a powerful influence on what is discussed in the counselling relationship. This can happen in a number of ways which I will consider in the following chapters. To illustrate my point about the impact of the context on counselling, I will consider the impact of the context's position with respect to the number of counselling sessions to be offered to clients on counselling.

The influence of context-specified length of counselling on what is discussed in counselling sessions

Imagine that a person (let's call her Susan) recognises that she has a problem and that she wants to seek counselling to address this concern. Susan has a choice of two counselling services in which to become a client. If she approaches 'Agency 1' counselling is free but she is limited to six sessions, while if she approaches 'Agency 2', counselling is time-unlimited, but she is expected to pay £25 per session.

If Susan chooses to be a client at Agency 1 then the chances are that she will helped to focus on her presenting problem and, if underlying issues come to the surface, the counsellor would pick them up but suggest that Susan may need to address them in a setting which is more open-ended with respect to time. By contrast, if Susan decided to become a client in Agency 2, she would be allowed much more opportunity to explore her concerns without the constraints of time being so pressing. As such, she may be able to identify and deal with any underlying problems that need to be addressed if she is to live resourcefully. Not that time unlimited counselling is without its problems, however. It may unwittingly encourage a client to avoid identifying or focusing on issues that need to be dealt with (since there is always time to do that later!) with the result that again the client may not be helped to live resourcefully.

My point here is that agencies that set a specified number of sessions influence the content of what is discussed in counselling for better or for worse.

The BACP definition of counselling

I mentioned at the beginning of this chapter that I would not be attempting to define counselling. Rather, I would outline a number of components that most people in the field would consider defining aspects of the counselling endeavour. I also said that while I would not define counselling myself, I would consider the current definition of counselling put out by the British Association for Counselling and Psychotherapy (BACP) published in November 2003. This definition is reprinted below:

'Counselling takes place when a counsellor sees a client in a private and confidential setting to explore a difficulty the client is having, distress they may be experiencing or perhaps their dissatisfaction with life or loss of a sense of direction and purpose. It is always at the request of the client as no one can properly be "sent" for counselling.

'By listening attentively and patiently the counsellor can begin to perceive the difficulties from the client's point of view and can help them see things more clearly, possibly from a different perspective. Counselling is a way of enabling choice or change or of reducing confusion. It does not involve giving advice or directing a client to take a particular course of action. Counsellors do not judge or exploit their clients in any way.

'In the counselling sessions the client can explore various aspects of their life and feelings, talking about them freely and openly in a way that is rarely possible with friend and family. Bottled up feelings such as anger, anxiety, grief and embarrassment can become very intense and counselling offers an opportunity to explore them, with the possibility of making them easier to understand. The counsellor will encourage the expression of feelings and as a result of their training will be able to accept and reflect the client's problems without becoming burdened by them.

'Acceptance and respect for the client are essentials for a counsellor and, as the relationship develops, so too does trust between counsellor and client, enabling the client to look at many aspects of their life, their relationships and themselves which they may not have considered or been able to face. The counsellor may help the client to examine in detail the behaviour or situations which are proving troublesome and to find an area where it would be possible to initiate some change as a start. The counsellor may help the client to look at the options open to them and help them to decide the best for them.'

I will now discuss the BACP definition of counselling in light of my component-based approach presented earlier in this chapter. Table 1.1 summarises the extent to which the BACP definition is reflected in my component-based approach, presented earlier in this chapter.

The BACP definition: the counsellor

As you can see from Table 1.1, the BACP definition of counselling focuses on certain aspects of what the counsellor brings to counselling (acceptance and respect for the client, the ability to listen attentively and patiently, and training which enables the counsellor to develop the personal strength of being able to accept and reflect the client's

Table 1.1 Elements of the BACP definition of counselling (right-hand column) to be found in Dryden's component-based analysis (left-hand column).

COUNSELLOR	
• A communicated genuine desire to be helpful	• Not mentioned
• A demonstrated acceptance and respect for clients	• Acceptance and respect for clients are essentials for the counsellor
• An ability to listen to and understand people's psychological pain from their perspective	• … by listening attentively and patiently, a counsellor can begin to perceive the difficulties from the client's point of view
• Excellent therapeutic communication skills	• Not mentioned
• Sufficient training	• … As a result of their training [the counsellor] will be able to accept and reflect the client's problems without being burdened by them
• Constructs to understand and to help	• Not mentioned
• Personal strengths and weaknesses	• [The counsellor is] able to accept and reflect the client's problems without being burdened by them
CLIENT	
• Personal pain	• Difficulty, distress, dissatisfaction with life, loss of a sense of direction and purpose
• Help-seeking by choice	• Always at the request of the client
• Ideas about being helped	• Not mentioned
• Personal issues affect behaviour in counselling	• Not mentioned
WORKING ALLIANCE	
• Bonds	• Do not judge or exploit clients
	• Acceptance and respect for clients
• Goals	• Enabling choice, change or reducing confusion

(Continued)

Table 1.1 *(Continued)*

• Tasks	***Therapist's tasks***
	• Explore client's difficulty, distress, dissatisfaction or loss of direction/purpose
	• Listen attentively and patiently
	• Perceive difficulties from client's point of view and help them to see things more clearly … possibly from a different perspective
	• No advice or directing client to take a particular course of action
	• Explore feelings with the possibility of making them easier to understand
	• Encourage expression of feelings (especially bottled-up feelings)
	• Able to accept and reflect the client's problems without being burdened by them
	• Enable client to look at many aspects of their life, their relationships and themselves which they may not have considered or been able to face before
	• Help the client to examine in detail the behaviour or situations which are proving troublesome and to find an area where it would be possible to initiate some change as a start
	• Help the client to look at the options open to them and help them to decide the best for them
	Client's tasks
	• Explore various aspects of their life and feelings, talk about them freely and openly
• Views	• Not mentioned
COUNSELLING AS AN ETHICAL ENTERPRISE	
• Informed consent	• Not mentioned
• Confidentiality	• Private and confidential setting
• Protection and development (supervision; personal work; CPD)	• Not mentioned
• **COUNSELLING AS A PROCESS**	• Development of trust

problems without being burdened by them), and neglects others (communicating a genuine desire to be helpful to clients, excellent therapeutic communication skills and a professional set of constructs to enable the counsellor to understand and help the client).

The BACP definition: the client

When it comes to what the client brings to counselling, the BACP definition acknowledges that they bring their personal pain and that they seek help by choice, but it does not mention that they bring their own ideas of being helped or that their personal issues are likely to be reflected in their in-session behaviour with their counsellor.

The BACP definition: the working alliance

When it comes to the working alliance between counsellor and client, the BACP definition does have something to say about the three aspects of the alliance outlined by Bordin (1979), that is, bonds goals and tasks, but it does not consider views, the fourth aspect introduced by me.

Bonds

When it comes to addressing the bond aspect of counselling, the BACP specifies two counsellor qualities that should be present: acceptance and respect for clients; and two which should be absent: judging and exploiting clients. Note that this definition addresses neither the client's contribution to the bond nor the interactive nature of the bond between client and counsellor.

Goals

The BACP definition does specify the goals of counselling, which it is says are to enable choice, change or to reduce confusion. While these are rather vague goals, they do address Mahrer's (1967) point that the goals of counselling are twofold: to overcome emotional disturbance (BACP's 'reduce confusion') and to promote growth (BACP's 'enable choice and change').

Tasks

As can be seen from Table 1.1, the BACP definition of counselling focuses heavily on the counsellor's tasks, almost to the exclusion of the tasks of the client, who is just asked to explore various aspects of their life and feelings and to talk about them freely and openly. Perhaps this imbalance is not surprising given that the BACP is attempting to define what the counsellor's tasks are, but it does tend to relegate the client to playing a bit part in the 'action' of counselling.

The BACP definition: counselling as an ethical enterprise

In my component analysis of counselling, I argued that there are three ethical domains to the counselling endeavour: informed consent, confidentiality and activities in which counsellors engage both to protect themselves and their clients and to further their own personal and professional development. Interestingly, the BACP definition just focuses on counselling taking place in a private and confidential setting and does not mention the two other ethical domains.

The BACP definition: counselling as a process

Earlier in this chapter, I argued that the process nature of counselling is one of its major components and I expand on this theme in the final chapter. The BACP definition of counselling does mention this subject, but only once and, in doing so, focuses on the development of trust between the counsellor and client as a hallmark of their developing relationship. In making this clear, the BACP definition also mentions that there are consequences of this development of trust: it enables clients to look at many aspects of their lives, their relationships and themselves which they may not have considered or been able to face. This shows the interactive nature of the components of counselling, a fact which should be borne in mind in the following chapters.

The BACP definition: the influence of context on counselling

As mentioned above, the BACP definition of counselling stresses that 'Counselling takes place when a counsellor sees a client in a private and confidential setting.' However, there is no other mention of the influence of context on counselling in the definition.

Having now considered one definition of counselling in depth, I will now clarify the nature of counselling by discussing what it does *not* involve.

What counselling is NOT

Another way of understanding counselling is to look at other helping activities that are typically not used by counsellors – to look at what counselling is not, as it were, and a number of writers on counselling have taken this approach. For example, here is Pete Sanders's (2002) view.

Counselling is NOT being a friend

Friendship has a mutual two-way focus which involves many different aspects, while counselling has a one-way focus on the well-being of one of the participants – the client. Friends go out together and go on holiday together. Counsellor and client decidedly do neither of these!

Counselling is NOT befriending

Befriending is different from friendship in that it is more of a one-way relationship, whereas friendship is two-way. While the befriending relationship is similar to counselling in that it is focused on the 'client's' well-being, it is dissimilar in that it has much looser boundaries than the counselling relationship. Thus, as a befriender you may well accompany the befriendee to social gatherings to offer company and immediate support, whereas you would not do this as a counsellor. The major goal of befriending is to help lessen the person's sense of social and personal isolation. In so doing, the befriender is prepared to be the *direct* source of the person's social contact. When counselling has the goal of lessening the client's sense of isolation, the counsellor aims to facilitate the client to find others in life to relate to, and will not aim to be the source of that contact.

Counselling does NOT involve caring in a parental way

Being a parent has a much greater involvement in the person's life than being a counsellor. In addition, being a parent often involves encouraging the person to do what the parent wants rather than what the person wants. This is not a part of counselling (or should not be!).

Counselling is NOT 'treating' or 'healing' like a doctor

Treating or healing implies the administration of a healing procedure by an expert to a person who passively receives it. Counselling involves the active involvement of the client and, while the counsellor has expertise, this is not used to get the person to accept passively what the counsellor says. Having said that, there are some counsellors who embrace the medical model and who talk of counselling as treatment.

Counselling is NOT instructing or teaching

Counsellors who are person-centred and psychodynamic would claim that they would not instruct or teach clients a body of knowledge or even skills to help themselves. These practitioners do not regard these activities as part of the counselling process. On the other hand, cognitive-behavioural counsellors would not hold this view. These practitioners argue that there is an important place in counselling for teaching their clients the cognitive-behavioural perspective on their problems and for instructing them in important self-help skills. This is one area in which CBT (cognitive-behavioural therapy) differs from person-centred and psychodynamic counselling.

Counselling does NOT involve guiding the client

Guidance involves giving a person access to accurate and appropriate information to help them make informed choices. It suggests that the helper is knowledgeable about where this accurate information is to be found, and most counsellors would not claim such expertise. On the other hand, other counsellors do have such expertise (for example, career counsellors) and as long as they help their clients (a) to explore the use of such information in a way that respects the clients and (b) to make the best choices for themselves, it is a moot point whether such guidance can be seen as part of counselling or as complementary to it.

Counselling is NOT advising

When advice is given – and assuming that it is well-meaning – it is usually given within the adviser's frame of reference. In other words, the adviser has a clear sense of what would benefit the advisee and advice is given to encourage the latter to do certain things that in the adviser's view will benefit the advisee. Advice frequently has under-tones of 'if I were you, I would …' Counsellors generally do not give advice, for two reasons. First, counsellors work within their clients' frame of reference rather than from their own. Thus, a course of action that may be right for the counsellor may not be right for the client. Secondly, advice-giving does little to encourage clients to think for themselves. What counsellors (at least from certain orientations) are prepared to do is to help their clients develop various ways of achiev-ing their goals and evaluate the advantages and disadvantages of each course of action so that they can choose the best course for them-selves. In advice-giving, advisers are basically using their brains; in counselling, counsellors encourage their clients to use their own brains. Thus counselling fosters client autonomy in ways that advice-giving generally does not.

Counselling is NOT just using counselling skills

Many professionals may use counselling skills in the course of their work, but this does not mean that they are engaged in counselling. Thus, when a nurse in the course of nursing a patient listens attentively and encourages that patient to express and clarify their fears, that nurse is not engaged in counselling; rather he or she is being a good nurse. Here the nurse is using skills that a counsellor would use, but is using them in the service of nursing. As Sanders (2002: 9) notes, when a professional such as a nurse, teacher or manager employs counselling skills it is 'in a manner consistent with goals and values … of the profession … in question'. He also notes that the use of such skills generally enhances the profession-specific skills of the practitioners in these professions. That is why I said that when the nurse in the above example uses counselling skills with the patient, he or she is being a good nurse. When a counsellor uses counselling skills, to use Sanders's words, it is in a manner consistent with the goals and values of the profession of counselling. From a person-centred perspective, how-ever, there tends to be an avoidance of the use of skills, but instead a strong focus on integrating the three core conditions as integrated attributes (Casemore, 2006, 2011).

Counselling is NOT life coaching

Since Sanders (2002) published his view on what counselling is not, life coaching has grown in popularity. In my view, while there are some similarities between counselling and life coaching in that they are both concerned with helping the client live more resourcefully, there are sufficient differences for me to state that counselling is not life coaching (a point also made by McMahon, 2005). Life coaching is a predominantly future-oriented form of helping where the focus is on helping the client to identify and work towards personal objectives. In general, lengthy discussion of the client's past is eschewed and if the client has a number of personal problems that impede him (in this case) from working towards his objectives then he is referred for counselling or psychotherapy. By contrast, while counselling can help the client to identify and work towards personal objectives this is not its only raison d'être. Counsellors will help the client to discuss what he wants to discuss, be it issues rooted in the past or present or likely to appear in the future. Counsellors will help the client discuss enduring emotional problems (whereas life coaches will not) and their training equips them to do so (whereas training for life coaching does not do so).

If we take a process view of counselling, then counsellors are more likely to help clients identify and work towards their personal objectives in the latter phase of counselling once the clients have sufficiently addressed their emotional problems to do so. It may be that CBT therapists are the group of counsellors most able to adopt the mantle of a coach at that time, given CBT's emphasis on specificity and goal-setting. Psychodynamic counsellors seem less comfortable in adopting a focused goal-setting approach (unless they are practising brief psychodynamic therapy) and person-centred counsellors will help their clients do so, particularly if the request to do so emanates from the client.

Segue

In this opening chapter, I have outlined and briefly discussed what I see as the components of counselling and considered these in the context of the latest definition of counselling published by the British Association of Counselling and Psychotherapy in November 2003. I also discussed the nature of counselling by considering several things that counselling is not. In the next chapter, I will amplify my view of the nature of counselling by considering the nature of the bonds between counsellors and clients.

Discussion issues

1 What are your views of the BACP definition of counselling?
2 What are your views of my component-based analysis of counselling?
3 How useful do you find the concept of the working alliance that I have presented in this chapter?
4 What are your personal strengths and weaknesses and how may these impact on your work as a counsellor?
5 In general terms, how do you think that the context in which you practise as a counsellor influences your work?

TWO

Bonds

'Bonds' concern matters to do with the relationship that develops between you and your clients. This relationship is considered in different ways by the different major counselling approaches, as we shall see later in this chapter. There are a number of components of the counselling bond that need to be considered. The first component has come to be known informally in the counselling world as the 'core conditions'.

The 'core conditions'

In the late 1950s, Carl Rogers (1957), the founder of person-centred counselling, wrote what has become perhaps one of the most quoted and influential articles that has ever been published in the counselling literature. His argument was that there were a small number of conditions that are necessary and sufficient for constructive personality change in clients to take place. This means that these conditions have to be present *and* that no others are needed for such change to occur. Over the years the terminology of these conditions has changed and there has been a lot of debate concerning how many conditions are deemed 'core', meaning necessary *and* sufficient. Most counsellors in the person-centred approach consider three such conditions to be core: empathy, respect and genuineness.

What is perhaps less well known about Rogers's (1957) thesis is that what makes these conditions necessary and sufficient is that *their presence has to be experienced by clients*. Quite a lot of research on these 'core conditions' was subsequently carried out concerning whether or not these conditions could be objectively and validly rated by independent observers. This led the focus to be on the contribution of counsellors (rather than on the clients' experience) and particularly on the relationship between counsellor-rated empathy and client outcome. However interesting such research was, it did not test Rogers's hypothesis: that it is the clients' *experience* of these conditions that is the main therapeutic ingredient. Let me now consider these conditions one at a time.

Empathy

If you are experienced as empathic by your clients then they will have a strong sense that you understand their experience from their point of view. For this to come about, you need to do the following. First, you need to understand in your own mind what your clients have been experiencing in their narrative accounts. Secondly, you need to communicate to your clients your understanding in such a way that they know ultimately that you are accurate in this understanding. Thus, you may understand in your own mind what your clients have been saying, but if you do not communicate this clearly, then your clients will not necessarily experience you as empathic. Thirdly, you need to retain your position as counsellor and not get overly involved emotionally in what your clients have been saying to you. This is known as the 'as if' quality of empathy, where you put yourself in your clients' shoes without wearing them, so to speak. If you fail to maintain this 'as if' quality in your work, then you will be at risk of burn-out and, more importantly, you will become overly involved with your clients, something that serves neither their healthy interests, nor yours.

I want to stress one point here. You don't always have to be accurate in your understanding of your clients right from the start, since this would give rise to an unhelpful perfectionism which has no place in counselling. Rather, you need to show that you keenly want to understand your clients and that you convey your attempts to understand in a tentative way so that your clients can experience your wish to understand and be able to correct you if you are wide of the mark. If you do this, you are also helping to develop a sense of teamwork between you and your clients, a quality that is generally regarded as therapeutic by all the main counselling approaches.

Respect

Much has been written on the ideal attitude that counsellors need to convey to their clients and that clients need to experience from their counsellors for counselling to be effective. Rogers (1957) originally called this attitude 'unconditional positive regard' (UPR),[1] a term which indicates two points: that you strive to show your clients positive regard and that you hold this attitude unconditionally. This is particularly challenging for counsellors who work with clients who exhibit gross anti-social behaviour, for example, and for this reason counsellors from all traditions are advised to work through personal issues that may prevent them from conveying UPR for their clients. The term 'unconditional positive regard' is a bit cumbersome and for a while Rogers referred to this condition as 'prizing'. To my knowledge he did not use the term 'unconditional prizing', and thus the status of the concept of unconditionality in this core condition is a little confusing. Latterly, person-centred counsellors refer to this core condition as 'respect' (rather than unconditional respect) and that is the term that I will use to describe this attitudinal condition. Once again, don't forget that what makes this condition therapeutic is not that you as counsellor feel respect for your clients, nor that you convey it to the satisfaction

---

[1]A condition that Rogers believed was an ideal to strive for, but could not be fully achieved (Casemore, personal communication).

of researchers. What makes this condition therapeutic is that your clients *experience* you as respecting them.

In the therapeutic approach that I practise – REBT (Rational Emotive Behaviour Therapy, located within the broad cognitive-behavioural tradition) – we strive to show our clients unconditional acceptance. First, note that the term 'unconditional' is used (as it was in Rogers's original term 'unconditional positive regard'), but that the term acceptance is employed instead of 'positive regard'. This term 'acceptance' is used in REBT theory to denote that a person is a highly complex mixture of positive, negative and neutral aspects and is certainly too complicated to merit a single evaluation (positive or negative) that completely accounts for him or her. REBT therapists would consider the term 'positive regard' as a positive evaluation of the whole person, and thus not as consistent with reality as is the term 'acceptance', with its emphasis on the complex mix of positive, negative and neutral features that make up a person. You may think that this difference in stance towards the client is a bit nit-picking and you may well be correct. But it does show that different therapeutic traditions have rather different ways of viewing the person.

Genuineness

When you are being genuine in the counselling relationship, you are being real in the sense that there is a consistency between how you feel, how you think and how you behave in the relationship. Many years ago, when I was at the beginning of my career as a counsellor, I witnessed a demonstration of counselling where, it seemed to me and the audience, the counsellor was demonstrating a high level of empathy for what the client was saying and a deep respect for the client. We were truly impressed. Imagine my shock therefore when after the demonstration was over I overheard the counsellor say in an aside to someone what a 'pain in the arse' the client must be to live with! He had kept this attitude well hidden from everyone, including the client, who commented in the post-interview analysis how she thought that the counsellor had demonstrated deep respect for her as a person.[2] This incident shows that a counsellor *can* be experienced as genuinely respectful by a client even when that counsellor is not being genuine. Whether counsellors can maintain such a non-genuine stance over time in the privacy of a consulting room is much more doubtful, and it is certainly not to be recommended. The counsellor in this demonstration was not being congruent in that his expressed attitude towards the client was very much at variance with his private attitude towards the person. The state of being in which one's inner and outer experience are the same is known as 'congruence', a term favoured by Rogers when he wrote his original 1957 paper.

At this point you may be thinking that it is possible to hold a hostile attitude towards a client and express that attitude to the client and be genuine or in a state of congruence. This is technically the case, but of course in this case your genuineness would not be therapeutic. This is why some people prefer the term 'therapeutic genuineness'. Others note that the core conditions need to be considered together, so that if you were congruent in expressing your hostile feelings towards one of your clients, you would neither be respecting the person nor likely to experience and convey an empathic understanding of their inner world.

How much should you reveal about yourself to your clients?

Different counselling approaches have different viewpoints on how much counsellors should reveal about themselves to their clients. In

---

[2] Another famous and quite relevant example of this kind of incongruence was former PM Gordon Brown's confrontation with the voter Gillian Duffy in Rochdale during the 2010 UK General Election: he appeared to listen to her sympathetically but later in his car, the mic on his lapel picked up his exasperated comment that she was a 'bigoted woman'.

Source: www.telegraph.co.uk/news/election-2010/7648327/General-Election-2010-Gordon-Browns-Gillian-Duffy-bigot-gaffe-may-cost-Labour.html the person-centred tradition, it is held that the person of the counsellor is the major source of therapeutic healing and thus the counsellor needs to be experienced as genuinely respectful and empathic in the therapeutic encounter if therapeutic change is to take place for the client. Here the view is very much that the counsellor cannot hide behind a role or count on the therapeutic value of techniques. If you are a person-centred counsellor the crucial variable is you and it is important that you reveal your feelings to your clients if they are sustained and are deemed to be helpful to your clients, or if they are getting in the way of your understanding your clients. The important factor here is that you reveal your feelings as they exist in the here-and-now context of the relationship. If you are a person-centred counsellor you do not, by and large, use your current feelings to explore the past experiences of your client. Rather you are keeping the focus on the immediate relationship between you and your client.

In other therapeutic approaches, the view of genuineness is different. For example, in psychodynamic counselling you would be encouraged to be genuine within the stance of neutrality, anonymity and abstinence (known collectively as the 'analytic attitude' – Lemma, 2003) that you would take towards your clients. The purpose of this analytic attitude is to encourage your clients to talk in an unfettered way about their concerns so that you may (a) discern and help them to see the relationship between their present conflicts and their past experiences if their problems are rooted in conflict and (b) help build up the functioning of their ego if their problems involve deficits. You would use your genuine responses to what they discuss to explore with them how they might be playing out these conflicts in their relationship with you or what thoughts and feelings they may be having that run alongside your own responses.

In cognitive-behaviour therapy, your genuineness underpins the technical nature of your counselling role and tends to have an educational aspect. For example, if I am trying to help a client understand the role that her thinking has on her anxiety about speaking in public, I may well reveal what I used to think when I was anxious about public speaking. This is known as self-disclosure, and tends to be more common in the person-centred and cognitive-behavioural approaches than in the psychodynamic approach.

Two unhelpful bonds

One way of looking at the core conditions is that when clients experience you as being empathic, respectful and genuine, then this is a very good sign that you are productively *involved* in a process that is therapeutic for your clients. I have stressed the word 'involved' here because there are two types of therapeutic involvement that are decidedly un-therapeutic and should be avoided. These are under-involvement and over-involvement. I will discuss both here as bonds that you should strive to avoid developing with your clients.

Under-involvement

If you are under-involved with some of your clients, you are unlikely to be helpful to them for a number of reasons. First, these clients, sensing your lack of involvement, may well not disclose themselves to you. Consequently, they will leave counselling sessions feeling frustrated and may well leave counselling altogether at a very early phase. Secondly, your clients may disclose themselves, but will fail to get an involved, therapeutic response from you. In this case, they may again leave counselling sessions feeling frustrated or thinking that there is something wrong with them that has led to their feelings being unacknowledged by you. Again, they may well terminate counselling early.

In one sense it is no bad thing for your clients to stop coming to see you if they experience you as uninvolved with them, particularly if they then go to see a counsellor who is able to be suitably involved with them. The problem, of course, is that your clients may well dismiss counselling as a potentially unhelpful process rather than conclude, more accurately, that you are not the right counsellor to help them.

If you are under-involved with some of your clients, then your relationship with those clients is characterised by one or more features.

- You fail, for whatever reason, to understand what your clients are saying, or, if you do understand, you fail to communicate this understanding in a way that your clients *experience* as empathic.
- You do not make your *presence* felt in the relationship. For whatever reason, you are unresponsive to your clients and your relationships with them are characterised by many silences which are not experienced as helpful by your clients.
- For whatever reason you find it difficult to experience respect for your clients. You thus do not feel a prizing for your clients who may well experience you as cold and disengaged.

One clue that you are under-involved with some of your clients is how you feel when you are waiting for them to arrive. If you are not looking forward to the sessions or if you are hoping that your clients will not turn up, then these are signs that you are under-involved with your clients. Another sign is that you suggest to your clients that you meet less frequently than is helpful for them.

If you are under-involved with some of your clients, then you need to do one or both of two things. First, you need to take your work with these clients to supervision as a matter of urgency and discuss the dynamics of these relationships with your supervisor. Secondly, you may need to discuss your feelings about your clients with your personal therapist. It may be that your lack of involvement with your clients reflects a personal issue that you need to explore and resolve if you are to be helpful to your clients. I will discuss this later in this chapter in the section on transference and counter-transference.

You may be seen to be under-involved with your clients when, in fact, this may not be the case. This is a particular issue for psychodynamic practitioners where adopting a less conversational silent stance is encouraged in order that clients with conflict-based problems may be helped to find themselves in the silence that can then ensue. This stance may be problematic with clients whose problems are deficit-based rather than conflict-based and who may find counsellor silence as evidence of lack of involvement. In working with such clients, Howard (personal communication) recommends that counsellors use silence more sparingly and be more responsive. In addition, Howard might indicate to such a client at a particularly vulnerable time that she is available to speak on the phone should the client need to. Howard notes that while clients rarely, if ever, take advantage of this opportunity, knowing that their counsellor is available counters the sense that that she is uninvolved with them in their hour of need.

The final counter to perceived counsellor under-involvement in psychodynamic counselling concerns helping clients with deficit-based problems deal with breaks. Some of these clients, who find it difficult to hold the counsellor as a symbolic object, experience breaks as being very difficult and Howard (2010) advocates on occasion that such clients take an object from her room to serve as a kind of transitional object, a reminder that she is still involved with them even in her absence.

Over-involvement

If you are over-involved with some of your clients you are likely bringing one or more unresolved personal issues to the counselling process. Typical reasons for over-involvement are as follows:

- You have a dire need to help your clients. One reason for this may be because you have invested your self-esteem in your clients' progress.
- You have a strong affinity for the client. This affinity may be sexual or non-sexual.
- You need your client to become dependent on you. This may be because you have invested your self-esteem in others being dependent on you.

Over-involvement with some of your clients means that you are again unlikely to be helpful to these clients. This is so for a number of reasons.

First, your over-involvement will interfere with your ability to listen to your clients from their perspective, because your listening will be contaminated by your own implicit personal agenda (as detailed above). For example, if you need your clients to make progress you will find it difficult to hear them when they say that they are not making such progress.

Secondly, you may inadvertently steer counselling sessions around to topics where you are overly involved with your clients. For example, if you are attracted to the lifestyle of one of your clients, you may encourage her (in this case) to talk about details of this lifestyle when it is not appropriate for you to do so.

Thirdly, you may encourage your clients to end counselling, or reduce the frequency of counselling sessions too soon. Thus, your clients may need further counselling despite making progress in one area, but you encourage them to go it alone, thinking that this proves that you have helped them. Your need to be helpful, in this case, has interfered with your therapeutic judgement.

Finally, you may discourage your clients from being their own counsellors when it is appropriate for them to do so, and encourage their reliance on your help. If you have based your self-esteem on the number of clients with whom you are working 'long-term', you will discourage clients who only need short-term help from leaving counselling.

If you are over-involved with some of your clients, then your relationship with those clients is characterised by one or more features.

- You spend a lot of counselling time socialising with your clients or discussing issues that you have brought up, rather than dealing with what your clients want to discuss.
- You over-emphasise your clients' gains and what they have achieved in counselling, and under-emphasise their problems and what they have not achieved.
- You make your *presence* felt too much in the relationship. As such you create the ethos that your contribution is crucial to your clients' development and you downplay their ability to help themselves.

Again, one clue that you are over-involved with some of your clients is how you feel when you are waiting for them to arrive. If you are unduly looking forward to the sessions or if you give your clients extra time when they do not need this, then these are signs that you are over-involved with them.

If you are over-involved with some of your clients, then again you need to take your work with these clients to supervision and discuss your feelings about them with your personal therapist, since your over-involvement with your clients probably reflects a personal issue that you need to explore and resolve if you are to be helpful to your clients (again see the section on transference and counter-transference later in this chapter).

It is important to distinguish between an over-involved relationship with clients and developing a capacity to relate at depth with them and be congruent in that relationship. The important marker here is the ability to sustain what Rogers (1961) called an 'as if' relationship with clients and what Casemore (2011) calls an attitude of clinical distance.

The bonds of influence

The discipline of social psychology suggests that it is possible to look at the counselling relationship as an interpersonal setting where influence takes place (Dorn, 1984). This perspective has not proven very popular with counsellors, who generally shy away from the idea that they influence their clients, preferring instead to see themselves as facilitating a constructive process that already exists within the clients. However unpalatable the 'counselling as influence' idea is to you, it is a useful way of understanding the bond between you and your clients. While I do appreciate that influence is a two-way process, I will focus here on the influence that you as counsellor have on your clients.

Most counsellors would agree with the idea that a major objective of the counselling process is to help the clients live a psychologically healthier life. This is implicit rather than explicit in the BACP definition of counselling discussed in Chapter 1, which argues that the counsellor's task is to encourage a client to pursue a course of action that is best for them from their own perspective. However, as counsellor you would respond very differently to a client with anorexia who wanted to gain weight and to look at reasons why she has used weight loss as a way of dealing with her distress, than to one who wanted to lose more weight. These different responses can be seen as different attempts to influence the client.

Although I am considering how you influence your clients, it is more accurate to say that clients allow themselves to be influenced by you. They do so for three major reasons:

1   Because they like you or find you attractive in some way. I am not primarily thinking of physical attractiveness here, although this may be the case.
2   Because they find you trustworthy.
3   Because they are impressed by your credibility as a counsellor. This may include your expertise and/or credentials.

Let me show you what I mean here. For Bill, a 30-year-old client, what matters is that he likes his counsellor. He had already consulted two well-known counsellors who had written widely and had national reputations, but he did not find them helpful. 'Although they had impeccable qualifications, I did not like them particularly, and thus what they said didn't really resonate with me,' he said. On the other hand, Bill found Mandy, a relatively inexperienced counsellor who had just qualified, much more helpful. 'I liked her and therefore I listened to her more,' he said.

Bill's responses are revealing and can be more widely applied. It is as if clients who have what we might call different influence preferences say the following:

•   I will listen to you and give credence to what you say if I like you.
•   I will listen to you and give credence to what you say if I trust you.
•   I will listen to you and give credence to what you say if I think you know what you are talking about.

My own experience as a counsellor, trainer and supervisor is that some clients may listen to, and allow themselves to be influenced by, counsellors whom they like but who do not show expertise, and others may listen to and allow themselves to be influenced by those who are expert, but whom they may not like. However, few clients will listen to counsellors whom they do not find trustworthy although they may like them or be impressed by their credentials.

One question that arises from this analysis is the following: To what extent should you as a counsellor find out which influence base your clients will best respond to and to what extent should you modify your approach to capitalise on this information? Thus, if you discover that one of your clients is most likely to listen to you if he (in this case) likes you, to what extent should you emphasise your likeability with this client? Conversely, if you discover that your client is most impressed by your credentials/expertise, to what extent should you emphasise these features in your counselling?

In an ideal world, clients would be impressed by the content of what you say irrespective of whether they like you or whether you have demonstrable expertise. However, in the real world of counselling, how the messenger is perceived often determines the potency of the message. My own answer to the questions that I have posed above is that you should endeavour to meet your clients' preferences on this matter to the extent that you are able to do so genuinely and to the extent that it is therapeutic for your clients for you to do so. I want to stress that this is my personal view and that other counsellors think differently about it. Here, as elsewhere, it is important that you think through the issues for yourself and arrive at your own conclusions.

Relational style

Your clients bring to counselling their own pre-existing tendencies to interact with people in certain ways. These styles are usually accompanied by ideas of how they expect other people to interact with them. A good working bond between you and your clients depends on the goodness of fit concerning your respective relational styles, assuming that such a fit is also therapeutic. On this latter point, it is possible for you and some of your clients to have a complementary relational style but for little effective therapeutic work to be done. Thus, you and one of your clients may both have an informal relational style, but spend your time discussing social matters rather than addressing important therapeutic issues. However, assuming that you and your clients do keep focused on the therapeutic task, what are good relational fits?

First of all, I do not believe that there is a universally good counsellor relational style. Indeed, the major therapeutic approaches recommend different counsellor relational styles, some advocating that the counsellor is active and directive in style (for example, CBT), with others proposing an active, non-directive attitude[3] (for example, person-centred counselling). Yet others favour a more passive, non-directive counselling style (psychodynamic counselling). Indeed, I have had many clients seek out CBT because they want their counsellor to be more active. I also know from my person-centred and psychodynamic colleagues that they have had clients seek them out because the clients wanted a less active or less directive counsellor. So, a good fit seems to be when the client is seeking a certain level of activity and direction from a counsellor and that counsellor provides it, while retaining a focus on the therapeutic task.

The task-focus/relationship-focus dimension

Another dimension of relational styles that is important to consider is what I call the task-focus/relationship-focus dimension. While all approaches to counselling acknowledge the importance of the relationship between you and your clients and the importance of engaging clients in the task-related work of counselling, the approaches place different degrees of emphasis on the relative importance of each. Thus,

---

[3]Casemore (personal communication) notes that it is not possible to be completely non-directive and that it is essential to develop a non-directive attitude that is marked by the avoidance of assuming the role of expert.

cognitive-behavioural counsellors recognise that the relationship between counsellor and client is important, but that what is more important in most cases is the client learning and implementing various tasks to deal with troublesome emotions and self-defeating behaviours. By contrast, person-centred counsellors argue that the quality of the relationship between counsellor and client is far more important than any tasks they engage in the counselling session. Psychodynamic counsellors tend to occupy the middle ground on this issue, although the relationship is more important in work with clients whose problems involve deficits than with those whose problems involve conflicts (Howard, 2010).

My point here is not to argue which approach is right or which stance I personally favour but to stress the goodness of fit between what you are offering and what your clients are seeking. My own practice tends to be more task-oriented than relationship-oriented, and I have often had people who have had a period of person-centred or psychodynamic counselling seek my help because they wanted to learn specific techniques to deal with their problems and they said that they did not learn such methods from their previous counselling. Conversely, I have referred clients to my person-centred or psychodynamic colleagues when it became clear that the clients wanted a more relationship-oriented mode of counselling than I practise. Here again, the importance is the goodness of fit between counsellor and client rather than the inherent superiority of one approach over another.

So far, I have focused on two dimensions: (1) level of counsellor activity and direction and (2) task/relationship focus. However, other styles are also salient, so let me discuss one further relational style dimension: formal/informal.

Formal and informal relational styles

When counselling is characterised by formality, modes of speech and address tend to be formal, physical distance between counsellor and client tends to be greater than when the relationship is more informal, and even dress tends to be more formal. Social niceties tend to be kept to a minimum and the more formal counsellors tend to reveal little about themselves. Conversely, when counselling is characterised by informality, modes of speech and address tend to be informal, physical distance between counsellor and client tends to be less than when the relationship is more formal and dress tends to be more informal. More informal counsellors are more likely to offer physical comfort where appropriate, and the degree of interpersonal warmth between the parties can be more readily discerned than in more formal counselling. Social niceties are more readily exchanged and counsellors may reveal more about themselves than more formal practitioners.

It may seem from this description that counselling is more task-focused when the bonds are more formal than when they are informal, but this is not the case. Counselling characterised by informality can be as task-focused as more formal counselling but it has a more relaxed 'feel' to it. Once again, counselling with a formal style is not inherently superior to counselling with an informal style (or vice versa), but the counselling process will be more smooth and probably more effective when the healthy style preferences of clients are met by the style of interaction provided by counsellors.

Counselling with respect to the formality of style tends to be ineffective when the formal style of the interaction between counsellors and clients is such that the counsellors fail to engage their clients in the *emotional* work of counselling. Here the work tends to be intellectual in tone with the result that the clients' emotions are peripherally engaged, if they are engaged at all. When counselling is informal, it is ineffective when this style leads to a chatty, social relationship developing between counsellors and their clients or when the counsellors fail to confront the clients appropriately.

Counsellors who place the *work* of counselling at the centre of the developing relationships that they have with their clients and engage them in a *bond* conducive to this work being carried out are to be emulated, since they are functioning well in both the bond and task domains of the working alliance.

Matching

Throughout this chapter, I have made the point that there is no particular bond that is therapeutic with all clients. Some clients work better with counsellors who are active and directive, while others do better with counsellors who are less active and less directive. Some gain more from counsellors with a formal style while others benefit from counsellors with a more informal relational style. It follows from this that there is some merit to matching counsellors and clients with respect to bond preferences and relational styles. Indeed, whenever I ask those who have referral responsibilities how they decide which clients to refer to which counsellors, they do mention factors such as personality and relational style. Speaking personally, I tend to get referred clients whom the referrer thinks need a robust and no-nonsense counsellor, rather than clients who need a lot of gentle coaxing. Psychodynamic counsellors would recognise this as the importance of providing 'paternal' interventions with clients whose problems are conflict-based, correspondingly providing 'maternal' interventions with clients whose problems are deficit-based where modulation of one's voice to the lower, softer regions may be a feature (Howard, personal communication).

The research literature on the concept of counsellor matching is suggestive of its benefits although the results are not clear-cut on this issue (Beutler and Harwood, 2000). It is useful for you to think carefully about your participation in the bond domain of the working alliance and in particular acknowledge areas of weakness of your work in this domain and attempt to address these weaknesses if they can be addressed. However, it is also important that you acknowledge that you cannot be all things to all clients and that your personality and temperament limit how much you can vary along the different bond dimensions that I have discussed in this chapter. Good counsellors know their own limitations and refer clients to other counsellors who may offer these clients a more productive bond.

Transference and counter-transference

The final aspect of the therapeutic bond that I wish to discuss concerns what are known in the psychodynamic counselling literature as transference and counter-transference. If we look at these concepts from a psychodynamic perspective, Howard (2006: 23) says that 'transference is the process by which we "transfer" onto the relationship with a counsellor our expectations about how we will behave with or experience other people and how they will behave or will experience us'. Counter-transference involves two possibilities: 'the first involves the therapist's transference to the client – in other words who the client represents in the therapist's inner world. The second takes as its starting point the client's transference and represents the therapist's unconscious response to it' (Howard, 2010: 72).

The idea that the relationship between you and your clients is coloured by your respective past relationships is a central idea in psychodynamic counselling. In this form of counselling, counsellors are actively looking for ways to help their clients gain insight into the relationship between their experience of their counsellor and their past interpersonal difficulties. They do so as a way of encouraging their clients to free themselves from these difficulties and react to the people in their current life in different, healthier ways. In cognitive-behavioural counselling, counsellors recognise transference reactions in their clients (without using such terminology) and help the clients to identify, examine and change the dysfunctional thinking that lies behind such reactions. In person-centred counselling, the focus is on clients' here-and-now experience of their relationship with their counsellors. The more the therapist is able to be real/genuine in the relationship, the more this will dissolve the transference. The more the therapist is transparent with their own feelings in the moment in the relationship, the more this will dissolve the counter-transference. Person-centred counsellors make little attempt to encourage their clients to reflect on the historical roots of their reactions unless the clients themselves bring up this issue.

Counsellors' experiences of and reactions to clients may also point to how these clients treat other people in their lives. This means that counsellors' reactions may provide useful information about the client. However, it may mean that these reactions are distortions of their clients stemming from unresolved issues in the counsellors' past. The three main approaches would acknowledge that both possibilities exist and what further unites these approaches is the recommendation that counsellors find a regular forum to explore their feelings about their clients either with their peers, supervisors and/or with their own personal therapists so that they can distinguish between healthy and unhealthy counter-transference reactions and take appropriate action.

The influence of context on bonds

I said in the opening chapter that the context in which counselling is practised influences that practice. The main impact that the context has on the relationships that counsellors form with their clients again concerns the time constraints that counselling agencies may place on their counsellors. While counsellors in brief counselling can and do form good relationships with their clients, the one thing that they cannot do in the time allocated to them is to develop the depth of relationships[4] that many clients do seem to need. What makes this issue particularly difficult is that it may not be apparent at an initial assessment which clients need a relationship of depth with their counsellors to gain lasting benefit from the counselling process. This is not to say

---

[4]See Mearns and Cooper (2005) for a full discussion of the concept of relational depth in counselling.

that longer is necessarily better in this respect. Just because a counsellor is working long-term with a client does not mean that she will inevitably develop a relationship of depth with that client. However, the opportunity to do so is there in long-term-counselling, whereas it is less likely to be present in time-constrained counselling.

In the next chapter, I consider those views that both counsellors and clients hold about counselling that have an impact on the process of counselling.

Discussion issues

1 Are you more prone to develop over-involved or under-involved relationships with some clients? What factors may be at play here?

2 To what extent do you vary your relational style with different clients? How would you explain your variations in style to your colleagues and to your supervisor?

3 In your counselling work how important are relationship factors as opposed to task factors? How would you explain this task–relationship balance to your colleagues and to your supervisor?

4 With what clients would you struggle to connect as you strive to develop a meaningful counselling relationship with them? What are the factors at play here?

5 What impact does the setting in which you practise as a counsellor have on the relationships that you develop with your clients?

THREE

Views[1]

Effective counselling, in my opinion, is based on a number of agreed understandings between you and your clients. If you both disagree on any aspect of the process, then a potential obstacle to the clients' progress exists and needs to be identified, explored and resolved. Such disagreements that you and your clients may have about counselling are often based on different views that you respectively hold about counselling. While Bordin (1979), the originator of the tripartite model of the working alliance that informs much of this book, did not put forward 'views' as a separate domain of the alliance, I have found it valuable to include it as such when reflecting on my own practice and as an aid in training and supervising counsellors.

In this chapter, I will discuss the most common of these views. Much of what I will discuss is based on the strong recommendation that you need to be explicit with your clients about the views that you hold about different aspects of counselling as a helping process, and that you need to encourage your clients to be explicit about their views as well. I further recommend that you engage your clients in an honest and open discussion of your respective views when these are at variance with one another. If these differing views cannot be reconciled and this fact makes counselling non-viable, at least this decision has been made on the explicit exchange of information. It is my contention that many counselling relationships founder on the rocks of unexpressed differing views, and whenever clients drop out of counselling it is worth keeping

[1]In this book, it is assumed that clients are deemed capable of making their own decisions (see Mental Capacity Act, 2005).

in mind that this may have been due to the fact that such clients held a different view from you about their problems or about some important aspect of the counselling process and that this difference was not brought out into the open.

Informed consent

Let me begin my discussion of the views domain of the working alliance by considering the principle of informed consent. Most codes of ethics and practice mention the importance of informed consent in the practice of counselling. By informed consent what is meant is that your clients give their consent to engage in salient aspects of the counselling process, having been informed about these aspects by you, their counsellor.

Thus, there are two aspects of the principle of informed consent: 'informed' and 'consent'.

But what should you inform your clients about? I think that clients need to be informed about and give consent to the following:

- the approach to counselling that you practise;
- the practicalities of counselling;
- confidentiality and its limits;
- the possible benefits and risks that the client may experience.

The approach to counselling that you practise

First, your clients need to be informed about the nature of the counselling that they are being offered. This does not mean that person-centred counsellors, for example, will give their clients a lecture on person-centred counselling (although some cognitive-behavioural counsellors might do this, for example Woods, 1991). What it means is that you will give your clients some indication about what counselling is likely to entail for them and what they can reasonably expect from you. Here, many counsellors would emphasise that their initial role is to listen to and strive to understand their clients from their perspective and that they are not there to give advice. Cognitive-behavioural counsellors would say that their additional tasks would be first to help their clients understand the role that thinking and behaviour plays in their problems and, secondly, to encourage them to stand back and examine such thoughts and behaviour with a view to changing them as a major way of enabling the clients to live more resourcefully.

How much information you provide clients concerning your approach to counselling is a delicate skill and one that will be influenced by a number of factors including:

1   *Your therapeutic approach's stance on the value of being explicit to clients about the nature of the approach.* Here cognitive-behavioural counsellors are likely to be more explicit than psychodynamic counsellors.
2   *The nature of the clients' problems.* It is easier to say how you might tackle some problems rather than others.
3   *The distress level of the clients.* It is not a good idea to inform clients about your counselling approach when they are very distressed.
4   *The intelligence level of the client.* Here it is important not to confuse some clients with information that is too complicated for these clients to process and not to patronise other clients by giving them simplified information when they are able to process more complicated material.

Here, as elsewhere, it is important to discuss such issues in training seminars and in supervision.

Here are three examples of counsellors from different orientation outlining their respective approaches to clients. First, Roger Casemore (2006: 2–4), the author of *Person-Centred Counselling in a Nutshell*, outlines person-centred counselling to one of his clients, Margaret.

'Well, Margaret, there are several different approaches to counselling in this country and I have been trained to work as a person-centred counsellor. There are some important differences between this approach and the other major approaches to counselling.

(Continued)

(Continued)

'First of all I have a very strong belief in the positive nature of all human beings. We will always strive to do the best for ourselves, no matter what conditions we find ourselves in or what problems we face.

'Secondly, I believe in the uniqueness and worth of every individual human being and that we all deserve respect for our capacity to choose our own directions in life and to select and choose our own values to live by.

'Thirdly, I believe that you are the only expert in your own internal world and the only person who really knows how you feel. You are the only person who can decide who and how you should be, the only person who can decide what the meaning of your life is and what you should do.

'Fourthly, I believe that the most important thing in counselling is the therapeutic relationship that will develop between us, in which I hope that you will really feel heard and understood, in a non-judgemental way and that you will experience me as a real and genuine person in this relationship. I will often be very open with my feelings as I experience them here, rather than playing the role of counsellor or expert whom you have come to see to ask for solutions to your problems.

'I am not an expert: I do not have any answers to your problems and difficulties. I believe that the answers to those, if there are any, lie within you. I will not probe or pry into anything you tell me, I will only work with what you choose to talk about. The only questions I will ask you will be to check out that I have heard and understood your feelings or to clarify the meaning of what you are telling me. I am quite used to a lot of silence and to tears and to other strong feelings being expressed.

'I will be very accepting of what you tell me and, at the same time, I will notice when the words you say seem to be at odds with how I am experiencing you. I might even notice these things out loud, like I did at the start of the session, when I saw that you seemed to be trying to look very calm and in control and yet there were lots of little signals that you were quite tense. I will do my best not to interpret anything you do or say with my meanings, but I will try to clarify what these things mean for you and how you are really feeling.

'I will try to be sensitive in what I say to you and at the same time I would want you to experience me as being really authentic with you and not putting on any pretence. I will be very direct and honest in sharing how I experience you and the things you talk about and you may find this way of working quite challenging at times.

'What I will try to do here, is to create a trusting relationship between us that will provide a safe space in which I hope you will feel accepted and understood so that you can be in touch with your feelings and talk, without fear, about anything which concerns you. I have a strong belief that we need to own and value all our feelings, even the most uncomfortable ones and to be able to say how we feel and to insist on being heard and understood. I hope that you will experience that here with me so that you will feel able to deal more effectively with the feelings that are troubling you.'

Second, here is how I explained the rational emotive behavioural approach to counselling to Kevin, one of my clients.

'Well, Kevin, there are a number of approaches to counselling and it is important that you understand something of the one that I practise which is known as Rational Emotive Behaviour Therapy (REBT). REBT is based on an old idea attributed to Epictetus, a Roman philosopher, who said that "Men are disturbed not by things, but by their views of things." In REBT, we have modified this and say that "People are disturbed not by things, but by their rigid and extreme views of things." Once they have disturbed themselves they then try to get rid of their disturbed feelings in ways that ultimately serve to maintain their problems.

'As an REBT therapist I will help you to identify, examine and change the rigid and extreme beliefs that we argue underpin your emotional problems and to develop alternative flexible and non-extreme beliefs. I will also help you to examine the ways in which you have tried to help yourself that haven't worked and encourage you to develop and practise more effective, longer-lasting strategies. At the beginning of counselling, we will consider your problems one at a time and I will teach you a framework which will help you to break down your problems into

(Continued)

(Continued)

their constituent parts. I will also teach you a variety of methods for examining and changing your rigid and extreme beliefs and a variety of methods to help you to consolidate and strengthen your alternative flexible and non-extreme beliefs. As therapy proceeds, I will help you to take increasing responsibility for using these methods and my ultimate aim is to help you to become your own therapist. As this happens, we will meet less frequently until you feel you can cope on your own.'

Finally, here is Susan Howard (2006: 4–6), author of *Psychodynamic Counselling in a Nutshell*, discussing the issue of informed consent and explaining psychodynamic counselling to clients in the context of her work with John, one of her clients.

'At this stage in his counselling John knew very little about psychodynamic counselling, what he might expect and whether this was the best approach for him. In reality he therefore did not know what he was agreeing to in saying he would come back to continue our conversation. Practitioners in other therapeutic models may at this stage endeavour to obtain formal informed consent from their client before proceeding further. By informed consent I mean that the client has sufficient relevant information about counselling to understand what he is agreeing to, including the nature, risks and benefits of the approach and the alternative approaches available. In common with many other psychodynamic practitioners I have not sought to gain informed consent at this stage and have not done so for a number of reasons.

'The major difficulty lies in the fact that until John has some experience of psychodynamic counselling he will be unable to know what he is consenting to. I could explain something of the nature of psychodynamic counselling to him, but it would probably not mean very much outside the context of experiencing it. Consent given at this stage may therefore not be truly "informed". At the same time there is a tension between giving John enough information to enable him to make an informed choice about continuing while not disrupting the nascent therapeutic relationship between us which will allow the emergence of unconscious material. As I said above, the therapeutic relationship is the central vehicle through which therapeutic change occurs, so my first task is to facilitate the development of that relationship. Often people in great distress do not want to hear about the advantages and disadvantages of a particular approach. They want their distress to be heard and taken seriously. Not to do so may inhibit the development of the relationship if the client feels that the counsellor is more concerned with her own agenda (to discuss risks and benefits) than his. Having said this, should a client ask about the nature, risks and benefits of counselling or other counselling approaches in the very early sessions, it should be discussed.

'Obtaining informed consent as soon as is practicable is a matter of good practice and I will need to address the issue with John at some point near the beginning of his counselling. The question is when? One way is to make a distinction between the assessment and "treatment" phases of counselling, and to discuss consent at the end of an assessment phase once John has had some experience of the approach so that he better understands what he is consenting to. To some extent making a distinction between assessment and treatment creates an artificial division, since psychodynamic practitioners argue that assessment is continuous and treatment begins the moment a client makes contact. However, it may be helpful to organise one's thinking around this division for the purpose of gaining informed consent.

'Not to gain his explicit consent means that I have assumed that John has given implicit consent to counselling by virtue of coming to see me. However, there are dangers in this, the most important of which is that John is vulnerable to commencing counselling without understanding the potential risks or difficulties involved. For example, many people who enter psychodynamic counselling find their relationships with important others in their lives change as they change, and this is likely to be true for John. Almost always this is generally for the better, but these changes can also involve losing friends or even a partner where the relationship has contributed to the emergence or maintenance of a client's distress. It is important that John understands these risks before he becomes too involved in the process of counselling.'

You might find it instructive to compare and contrast these different perspectives on explaining counselling to clients and reflect on their respective strengths and weaknesses.

The practicalities of counselling

The second area of counselling that you need to be clear about at the outset concerns what might be called the practicalities of counselling. These include:

- the length of counselling sessions;
- your fee, if any is being levied;
- your cancellation policy – particularly in relation to the payment of a fee if a session is not cancelled within the specified period; and
- how your clients can contact you, and the limits of such contact.

The importance of being explicit to clients about the practicalities of counselling can be illustrated in a recent episode from my own caseload. One of my ongoing clients was involved in a romantic relationship which had started to go wrong and she asked whether I would see her together with her boyfriend for couple therapy. I said that this was not a good idea since I had been seeing her for a couple of years and that the boyfriend, who was ambivalent about couple therapy, might think that I was biased in favour of my client because I had an established counselling relationship with her. However, I did refer them to a colleague who has a good reputation in working with couples. I mentioned that his fee might be somewhat higher than mine. My client and her partner subsequently saw my colleague for two sessions. When she received his invoice, my client was very angry and refused to go back. While she was expecting to pay a fee somewhat larger than mine she was not expecting his fee to be three times higher than mine! This very experienced practitioner had not made his fee explicit at the outset and this omission led to the early dissolution of the therapy.

If you and your clients disagree about any of the practicalities of counselling then these disagreements need to be resolved before counselling begins. Otherwise, it cannot be said that your clients have given informed consent to proceed.

Confidentiality and its limits

It is often stressed that counselling is a confidential process. This means that you will not disclose confidences entrusted to you by your clients to any third party. However, in counselling there do exist limits to absolute confidentiality and these need to be made clear to clients before counselling gets under way so that they can give their informed consent to proceed. Here are some of the exceptions to absolute confidentiality:

1   You will inform a relevant third party if one of your clients poses a significant risk to her (in this case) own life and will not take steps on her own behalf to protect herself.
2   You will inform a third person if one of your clients poses a significant risk to the life or well-being (especially in the case where minors are involved) of another person or other people.
3   If you work in a setting where reports of counselling sessions to other relevant professionals are required, then you will provide such reports.
4   If your clients' counselling is being paid for by a private insurance company, it is likely that you will have to provide this company with periodic reports of the counselling if payment is to be renewed.
5   If you are making digital voice recordings counselling sessions (for example, to fulfil the requirements of a training course), it may be that other people will listen to these recordings. Thus, the use of these recordings should be made clear concerning who is to listen to them and why, as well as their ultimate fate.
6   You will take appropriate legal steps to recover your rightful fees if one of your clients has persistently and unreasonably refused to pay such fees.
7   You are legally required to provide notes of counselling sessions on proper request from the courts.

The possible benefits and risks of counselling

A number of clients want to know at the outset what benefits they can expect from counselling. This is a difficult issue to deal with since while you will wish to engender hope in your clients by stressing the possible benefits, you will not want to promise what you cannot deliver. With respect to the latter point, my personal experience is that some clients, who have heard that CBT is a brief intervention, expect to be significantly helped with their long-standing chronic problems in a short period of time. My response is to say that while CBT can be short-term, it can also be a longer-term intervention and I will be better placed to offer an opinion on the amount of time I will need to help the client with her problems once I have understood more fully their nature and how she responds to CBT. I think that this approach indicates that the answer to the benefits question will emerge during the process of counselling without engendering false hope in clients.

Counselling has its risks[2] and I agree with Howard (2010: 55) who says the following: 'I do also give a "health warning" around relationships, that there may be unpredictable changes as therapy progresses. Clients have often said to me later that they have appreciated the warning when relationships changed, particularly when they become more difficult.'

What type of informed consent is elicited?

Some counsellors favour providing clients with a written outline of information about the approach to counselling being provided, the practicalities of counselling, the limits to absolute confidentiality and other relevant information. A good example of such a written outline is presented in Appendix 1 (pp. 121–6).

---

[2]See Reeves (2010) for how to respond when your client is at risk of suicide or self-harm.

In addition to providing such written information some practitioners require their clients to sign a form to indicate informed consent. This is referred to as a counselling contract. Other counsellors prefer to give relevant information verbally and are prepared to accept a verbal informed consent from their clients. Whichever approach you take, being explicit about such matters and gaining clients' informed consent on these points is not only ethical, it is a mark of good practice and strengthens the working alliance between you and your clients.

Some social workers in the USA make an interesting distinction between an 'applicant' and a 'client' (Garvin and Seabury, 1997). They argue that when a person has given informed consent to proceed with counselling he or she becomes a client. Until that point the person is an applicant for help. You might find this distinction useful in your own work.

Views on client problems

I have argued above that one of the initial tasks you have as a counsellor is to give your clients a brief outline of the counselling approach that you practise. This is likely to be put in general terms and tailored according to what your clients are likely to understand and digest. Since clients have not begun to discuss their concerns in any significant detail, you will not have had an opportunity to gain an in-depth understanding of their problems and will thus not have had the opportunity to convey to the clients your detailed understanding of their problems, informed as it is by the professional constructs of the approach to counselling that you practise. Once your clients have had such an opportunity to disclose and explore their concerns, you are in a better position to convey to them your professional understanding of their problems.

Having said this, some counsellors in the course of outlining their approach to counselling make reference in general terms to how they make sense of clients' problems. Notice how I did this with

Kevin (see pp. 49–50). I said that according to REBT: 'People are disturbed not by things, but by their rigid and extreme views of things', and that, 'Once they have disturbed themselves they then try to get rid of their disturbed feelings in ways that ultimately serve to maintain their problems.' Compare this to Roger Casemore's statement to Margaret (see pp. 47–9) which does not make any reference to how he as a person-centred counsellor makes sense of clients' problems in general. According to Casemore (personal communication) it is not the person-centred counsellor's job to make sense of the client's problems, but to get an understanding of how the client experiences their problems from their frame of reference.

Different counselling approaches make different recommendations concerning how explicit counsellors should be in sharing their conceptualisations. Most (but not all) cognitive-behavioural counsellors will tend to be very explicit about the way they conceptualise their clients' problems, often using with their clients the professional constructs that they use with one another, arguing that it is centrally important to agree a shared understanding of these problems before appropriate treatment strategies are formulated. On the other hand, psychodynamic counsellors tend to avoid making explicit the professional constructs that guide their understanding of their clients' problems, fearing that doing so will encourage their clients to intellectualise their problems and to use such a mechanism as a defence against the feelings engendered by these problems. What they will do is to make interpretations of the meaning behind their clients' communications. These interpretations seek to help clients to gain an understanding of the hidden forces driving their problems, and as such are problem conceptualisations of a sort, but they emphatically do not constitute the counsellors' professional understanding of the clients' problems. Thus, where REBT counsellors may well use the term 'irrational beliefs' in outlining their understanding their clients' problems (explaining carefully what they mean by such terminology), psychodynamic counsellors will rarely, if ever, use such professional terms as 'Oedipal conflict' with their clients. Person-centred counsellors tend, in my experience, to occupy a middle ground and will share their professional conceptualisations when requested to by their clients and when such requests are experienced as legitimate requests for information.

From a working alliance perspective, explicitly sharing your views about your clients' problems has two main advantages. First, it promotes clearer communication between you and your clients and keeps misunderstandings to a minimum and, secondly, it enables your clients explicitly to give their informed consent to proceed, based on a clear understanding of how you as a counsellor understand their problems.

On the other hand, you and your client may share a common conceptualisation of the latter's problems at an implicit level and therefore there is no need for you to make this issue explicit, as it would seem like stating the obvious. My own concern about this stance is that it depends very much on the accuracy of your inference about your client's level of agreement. Your inference may be wrong, even though you may 'feel' that it is correct. However, please bear in mind that this preference for explicit communication reflects my cognitive-behavioural approach in which explicit communication is favoured over implicit communication.

Barker et al. (1990) have done some interesting research on clients' views of their problems and the impact that these subsequently have on counselling, and I recommend that you look at this research if you are interesting in learning more about this issue.

Views on treatment

I have already made the point in this chapter that you should preferably outline the way you practise so that your clients can make an informed decision about whether they wish to avail themselves of this kind of help. I also provided three examples of how counsellors from three different traditions approach this task.

You will note from what I said to Kevin about REBT that I was quite explicit both about how REBT conceptualises clients' problems and how it approaches their remediation. Indeed, I hope you can see how my statement about therapy followed logically from my statement concerning problem conceptualisation. This is not the case in Roger Casemore's communication to his client, Margaret. Roger does not say much about how person-centred counselling conceptualises client problems. Instead, Casemore (2011) argues that the person-centred counsellor should work at getting an agreed formulation with the client and to do this in a way that is congruent with the person-centred ethos that eschews the use of professional jargon in problem conceptualisation. What Roger does is to focus on the conditions that he will endeavour to create in his work with Margaret, a stance that is highly consistent with the emphasis placed in person-centred counselling on the role of the core conditions in counselling (see Casemore, 2006). Thus, some counsellors make an explicit link between conceptualisation and treatment in making their views clear about how they practise, and other counsellors do not.

From a working alliance perspective, what is important is that you and your client agree on how you are to approach dealing with the latter's problems. Effective counselling is much more likely to proceed when the two protagonists agree on this issue than when they do not.

On what issues should you and your clients agree with respect to how the clients' problems are to be addressed, leaving aside the question of whether such agreements should be explicitly or implicitly made?

As I have already said, ideally you and your clients should agree broadly on how you both understand the clients' problems and how these problems should be tackled. If we examine this second issue we see that agreements are desirable concerning what you are to do and what your clients are to do in addressing their problems. These are known respectively as the counsellor's tasks and the client's tasks, and I will discuss these in greater depth in Chapter 5. What I want to concentrate on here are the views that you and your clients hold about one another's tasks.

Throughout this chapter, I have stressed how important it is for you to gain informed consent from your clients. This involves you doing the following:

- giving some form of explanation about counselling;
- checking that your clients have understood this explanation;
- discussing any issues that the clients have about this explanation;
- clarifying any aspects of the explanation that the clients have not fully grasped;
- eliciting the clients' consent to proceed with counselling based on their accurate understanding of the explanation.

Let me illustrate how I implemented this sequence with one of my clients, Lisa, as I discussed how I saw my tasks and her tasks in counselling. Remember that my therapeutic orientation is Rational Emotive Behaviour Therapy (REBT), a form of cognitive-behaviour therapy (CBT) where explicit communication is particularly valued, and as such I am not claiming that this is *the* way of outlining the counsellors' and clients' tasks, only *one* way of doing so.

Windy: Before you decide whether you want to work with me in counselling, would it be useful if I outlined in a little more detail the way I practise and what this implies for you as a client in this form of therapy?

Lisa: Yes, that would be useful.

Windy: OK. Well, I see my major tasks as follows. First, I will help you to specify your problems and find out from you what you would like to achieve in addressing each problem. Then we will work on your problems initially, one at a time, and as we do so I will outline a framework that will help both of us understand the major unhelpful beliefs that underpin your problems and the ways in which you unwittingly maintain these problems. If that framework makes sense to you I will teach you how to use it for yourself. Any questions so far?

Lisa: Well, what if this framework doesn't make sense to me?

Windy: If that happens, we will discuss this and it may be that you will find another approach to counselling more helpful to you. If so, I will be happy to refer you to a practitioner of an approach that will suit you best.

Lisa: Fine.

Windy: OK. Now, once I have taught you this assessment framework, my next major role is to help you both to stand back and re-evaluate the unhelpful beliefs that underpin your problems and to develop healthier beliefs that will enable you to achieve your therapeutic goals. Then, most of my work will be to encourage you to practise and strengthen these healthy beliefs and deal with any obstacles along the way. Throughout, I will be teaching you new skills that will enable you to be your own therapist and as we go on I will encourage you to take increasing responsibility in assessing and dealing with your own problems. I will also help you to generalise to other problems the gains that you have made.

Lisa: So you will be expecting a lot from me!

Windy: Well, we are a team. I have tasks to perform and so do you. How do you feel about that?

Lisa: It's a bit daunting. I thought all I would have to do is to come once a week and talk about my problems.

Windy: OK, let me put it like this. Imagine you wanted to play the piano and you came to me for lessons. Would you expect that all you had to do was to practise what I taught you here?

Lisa: No, that would be silly. I see what you mean. I have to practise outside counselling what you teach me inside counselling.

Windy: I couldn't have put it better. As we are talking about your role in the process, let me outline what I see as your tasks and then we can talk about them. OK?

Lisa: Fine.

Windy: Well, first I expect you to be as honest as you can about your problems and specify them as best you can. I will help you to do this. Then, I expect you to be open-minded when I outline the framework that is a central part of this approach to counselling, that is, that the way we feel and act is based largely on the way we think about things and that our problems are based on rigid and extreme beliefs. I don't expect you to swallow everything that I say uncritically. Far from it. Indeed I expect you to raise any doubts, reservations and objections that you have about this framework and anything else that I might outline to you. Is that OK?

Lisa: Oh, that's good. So I can challenge you if I don't agree with you.

Windy: Most certainly. I actively encourage you to do so. Then, if you find the framework helpful to you, I expect you to use it both as a way of making sense of your own problems for yourself outside counselling sessions and as a way of structuring what we talk about inside these sessions. The same applies to the skills that I will teach you that will enable you to re-evaluate your unhealthy beliefs and to strengthen their healthy alternatives in your everyday life. As you noted yourself earlier, if you wanted to learn how to play the piano you would have to practise between lessons. The same is true in this form of counselling. You get out of it largely what you put into it.

Lisa: So, do I do what you tell me to do between sessions?

Windy: Not at all. We will work out together what you will do between sessions, based largely on what we have discussed within the sessions. Once we have agreed on what you will do, I expect you to do it and if you experience any problems in so doing we will talk about these problems at the following session. Change is rarely smooth, so a lot of counselling is about identifying and dealing with obstacles to change.

Lisa: Sounds a difficult process.

Windy: Well, it can be. I often put it like this. Everything that I teach you in counselling is simple, very little is easy to apply. However, if you are willing to commit yourself to carrying out your tasks and if I carry out my tasks to the best of my professional ability, together we will make a powerful team in helping you to address your problems and to achieve your goals. How does that sound?

Lisa: It sounds realistic but hopeful.

The final issue that I want to discuss in this section on views of treatment from a working alliance perspective concerns the length of counselling.

Some research has shown that clients often expect counselling to be a far briefer intervention than do their counsellors (Maluccio, 1979). If the length of counselling is not discussed and made explicit, then the failure to do so can pose a serious threat to the working alliance. I will raise this issue with my clients if they do not do so at the outset. My own experience as a counsellor is that clients often ask the question about treatment length at a very early stage, before I can realistically answer it. Thus, when a person first rings me about the possibility of my taking them on for counselling, he or she will ask me how long therapy will last. At this point, I know very little or nothing about them, the nature of their problems or what they want to achieve from counselling. Consequently, I am in no position to offer an informed opinion on this issue. Therefore, I will say that I *will* answer their question, but only when I am in a position to do so. I am generally willing to say how much time I will need with a person, once I know the following:

- *The number and nature of the problems that they wish to discuss with me.* In general, the greater the number of problems clients have and the more complex these problems are, the longer they will need to be in counselling.
- *What they want to achieve from counselling.* In general, the more ambitious the clients' goals, the longer they will need to be in counselling.
- *How acute or chronic the clients' problems are.* In general, the more chronic the clients' problems, the longer they will need to be in counselling.
- *How mentally healthy the person is.* In general, the more mentally healthy the clients are, the less time they will need to be in counselling.

Having said this, the main point is that you and your clients should negotiate the length of counselling when you both are in a position to do so, bearing in mind that this may need to be renegotiated once counselling is under way. Many counsellors suggest an initial period of counselling for their clients to experience the process and then review that experience before agreeing on a suitable length of treatment.

As I said above, problems can arise when you and your clients have different ideas about the length of counselling. This may be a particular issue for cognitive-behavioural counsellors, like myself, who are consulted by clients with multiple, complex, chronic problems for whom long-term therapy is indicated, but who have sought CBT precisely because they have heard that it is a short-term approach. Now CBT *can* be a short-term therapy with people who are basically mentally healthy, but who have one or two acute, specific problems. However, with those who have more complex, multiple, problems and who have a personality disorder, longer-term CBT is indicated, particularly if their goals are ambitious.

The impact of context on views

How might the context in which counselling takes place have an impact of the views that counsellors and clients have about salient aspects of the counselling process? Some clients seek counselling quite explicitly from an organisation where a particular view of counselling resonates with the clients' views. For example, Maggie was depressed after having been made redundant from her job. She sought counselling from an organisation that made explicit the spiritual dimension of client problems and how they are best tackled. Thus, Maggie and her counsellor had an agreed view of the nature of her problems (namely that the loss of her job had triggered a spiritual void in Maggie's life which needed to be explored within a spiritual frame of reference). When Harry sought counselling from the same organisation, he did not know its spiritual emphasis and being a 'down-to-earth, dyed-in-the-wool atheist' did not resonate with his counsellor's spiritual view of his problems and how they best needed to be tackled. Harry dropped out of counselling at the end of the second session, complaining that his counsellor was 'too airy fairy' and benefited from a problem-oriented counsellor who worked in his GP practice.

Thus, counselling in an agency that emphasises the importance of the spiritual dimension of life is likely to be different from counselling in an agency that offers time-limited CBT. The difference is likely to be occur in how clients' problems are conceptualised and how 'treatment' is viewed. From a working alliance perspective, the one agency is not better than the other. Rather, as the cases of Maureen and Harry show, the degree of agreement between the views of the counsellor (as representative of the agency) and those of the client needs to be strong enough to allow productive counselling work to ensue.

In the next chapter, I will consider the goals domain of the working alliance.

Discussion issues

1 How do you approach eliciting informed consent from your clients?
2 In what ways do you convey to your clients how you conceptualise their problems?
3 In what ways do you convey to your clients how you intend to work with them on their problems?
4 How do you deal with cases when your clients disagree with your views on their problems and/or how to work with them on these problems?
5 What influence does the context in which you work as a counsellor have on your views of your clients' problems and of how you can work with them therapeutically?

FOUR

Goals

So far I have discussed matters that relate to the bonds that develop between counsellors and clients and those that relate to how both view counselling and its various aspects. In this chapter, I will concentrate on a third domain of the working alliance: goals.

As Alfred Adler (1979) pointed out many years ago, all human endeavour has a purpose. So when your clients seek help from you each one has an idea about what they want to achieve from the meetings. These goals may be explicitly stated at some point in the process or they may remain implicit. Whichever is the case, these goals are inherent in the process in counselling. In this chapter, I will discuss the goals of counselling, initially concentrating on selected issues concerning the goals themselves before looking at goals from a working alliance perspective. A full discussion of goals in counselling merits its own separate volume.

Your clients' goals

Your clients come to see you for a variety of reasons but what unites their purpose is that they are suffering in some way and come to you because they are hopeful that you may help them over their suffering. This obvious truth obscures a number of important questions. For example: What does it mean to be 'over' one's suffering? And what does your client want to achieve from counselling?

The relationship between your clients' problems and goals and the level of specificity of each

One way of looking at clients' goals is to consider them in relation to the problems for which they are seeking help. You can do this if your clients' problems are specific, or if they are general. Let me first consider the case when your one of your clients has a problem that is specific in nature. Thus, if a client comes to you because she (in this case) is experiencing anxiety about speaking in public to the extent that she avoids doing so, then you can ask her a goal-oriented question such as: 'What would you like to achieve from counselling with respect to this problem?' In response to this your client is likely to give you a fairly specific answer, such as: 'I want to be able to speak in public without feeling anxious', a response which relates your client's goal to her problem in a fairly clear way.

If your client's problem is more general (for example, 'I just feel empty inside most of the time') you can still ask the same question as before, namely: 'What would like to achieve from counselling?' However, you may well get a response that is general in nature (for example, 'I just want to feel my old self again'). This shows that the more specific clients' problems are, the more specific their counselling goals are likely to be.

Counsellors from different orientations have different stances towards client goals. For example, cognitive-behavioural counsellors are more goal-oriented than counsellors from the other two major approaches (that is, psychodynamic and person-centred) and when their clients disclose problems that are vague or general in nature, they work hard to help the clients to put these problems into more specific terms. When they have done so, the counsellors then help clients to be as specific as possible about their goal in relation to each specified problem.

Psychodynamic counsellors, by contrast, may not focus very much on helping their clients to articulate their goals, believing that doing so, particularly at the outset, may inhibit the clients' exploration. Having said this time-limited psychodynamic counselling is more goal-oriented than longer-term psychodynamic work. But even here, client goals are more likely to be broader than goals negotiated in CBT (e.g. 'To get back to work' and 'To make a decision about staying with or leaving my husband').

Person-centred counsellors would avoid being problem-oriented, goal-centred or solution-focused; rather, the emphasis would be on maintaining a relationship in which the client can choose to identify goals and how they wish to work on them (Casemore, personal communication).

Your clients' presenting problems and goals

You may have heard the term 'presenting problem' in your training. It refers to the initial problems clients present with in counselling. These may be significant and represent what clients are most concerned about, and when this is the case it is appropriate for you to set goals (if this is your practice) and focus your work on these problems and goals. However, presenting problems may not be as significant as other problems clients may have. The disclosure of these presenting problems may be used by clients to test the water – i.e. to see what counselling is like – or as a test of trust (Fong and Gresback Cox, 1983) – i.e. to see if you as a counsellor are trustworthy or competent before more significant problems are revealed. If the client's presenting problems are not as significant as their other problems it would not be appropriate to set goals with respect to these problems and focus your work on these problems/goals, since doing so might well inhibit the disclosure of the client's more significant problems.

You are probably thinking: 'How do I know if a particular client's presenting problem is significant or not?' A full answer to this question is beyond the scope of this volume, but let me make the following observations:

- Avoid taking extreme positions on this issue (namely, that a client's presenting problem is either always significant or never significant).
- A presenting problem is significant if the client is clearly upset when discussing it and when the client frequently returns to the problem.
- Discuss this issue with your counselling supervisor.

Whether your clients' presenting problems are significant or not, it is important that you take them seriously and respond empathically to your clients when they are discussing these problems. Doing so will encourage your clients to disclose deeper, more significant problems, should these exist.

Are your clients' goals internal or external?

When you ask your clients what they want to achieve from counselling, their responses will reveal whether their goals are internal or external. Internal goals concern that which your clients have direct control over, which are broadly their own psychological processes – namely, their thoughts, feelings and behaviour. External goals, on the other hand, concern that which your clients would like to have direct control over, but do not – namely, other people's thoughts, feelings and behaviour and the external environment. This is not to say that your clients cannot influence others and the external environment, but they exercise their influence through their own behaviour, over which they do exercise a large measure of control. Consequently, when your clients reveal external goals, your task is to find a way of showing them why you cannot accept such goals for change and to help them to set internal goals for change. How you choose do this will depend on the theoretical orientation of your counselling approach. My own (CBT-oriented) practice is to explain this issue directly to my clients when relevant and then to work with their responses.

Are your clients' goals realistic (achievable) or unrealistic (unachievable)?

Once your clients have set internal goals there arises the question of whether these goals are realistic or unrealistic. Realistic goals are basically goals that are achievable, whereas unrealistic goals are basically unachievable. Unrealistic goals tend to be perfectionist in nature and usually serve to maintain clients' problems. An example of an unrealistic goal is when clients say that they no longer want to feel a disturbed emotion that they have been struggling with. Thus, it is common for clients to say that they no longer want to feel anxious or depressed. Now, it is inhuman never to be anxious or depressed. While all humans feel anxious in the face of threat and depressed in response to a significant loss, it is realistic for clients to feel such emotions and use them as a cue to deal with the threats and losses in more effective ways, rather than be stuck with these feelings and be unable to move on. On the other hand, it is unrealistic for them never to feel such emotions at all. So when clients set such unrealistic goals, you need to find some way of broaching this subject with them.

Whose goals are being expressed?

When you ask your clients what they want to achieve from counselling, it is important that you bear in mind that their response might indicate what other people want them to achieve from counselling, or what they 'should' want to achieve, rather than what they truly do want to achieve in their heart of hearts. When clients have indicated what their counselling goals are, I find it useful to ask them who else wants them to achieve these goals. When they have nominated the relevant people, I ask the following question: 'If these people were unconcerned about what you were to achieve from counselling or if they wanted you to achieve the opposite, would your goals still be the same?' If the clients say that their goals would be the same, then you can be reasonably certain that your clients' goals are truly their own. Whereas, if they prevaricate in their answer or say outright that their goals would change, then this indicates that their stated goals may not be their own. If this is the case, then you have a very useful area to pursue concerning the role of others in the clients' life.

Your clients' goals can be based on psychological disturbance

When you ask your clients what they want to achieve from counselling, bear in mind that their goals may be based on their problems rather than on a healthy vision of what is in their best interests. An obvious example, but one which makes the point, concerns young women who suffer from anorexia. If you ask them what they want to achieve from counselling they may respond that they would like to lose more weight. This stated goal is quite clearly unhealthy and is based on the clients' problems, and if you help them to work towards such a goal you are helping your clients to get worse. In such circumstances, you need to find a way of discussing this issue with your client without making them defensive. Helping your clients to stand back and evaluate their goals when these are based on problems, rather than representing solutions to these problems, is a complex skill and one which requires close training and supervision.

Greenberg (2002) argues that the best time to ask a client about her goals is when she is in what he calls her 'maladaptive state' (a disturbed state of mind). He recommends asking the question: 'What do you need when you feel like this?' as a way of accessing meaningful goals. He says: 'People, when they are suffering and in pain, usually know what they need' (Greenberg, 2002: 194).

These seemingly different views can be reconciled as follows. It is important to distinguish a client's short-term goals when she is in a 'maladaptive state' (e.g. 'I need comfort when I am in pain') and her longer-term goals which may be better accessed when the person is not in that state (e.g. 'I need to assert myself with my partner when he puts me down').

This discussion does point to the importance of having an objective and open mind when exploring goals with a client who is in a psychologically disturbed or maladaptive state.

Your clients' stated goals: are they real or not?

I introduced you to the idea of stated goals in the above section. As the term suggests, stated goals are goals that your clients state that they want to achieve from counselling. Now, just because one of your clients states that she wants to achieve 'X' from counselling, it does not follow that 'X' is what your client truly wants to achieve. The following are reasons why stated goals might not reflect your clients' true goals.

1   Your clients may be ambivalent about their goals but may not express their ambivalence. They only state the goal, not the fact that they are in two minds about it. If you suspect that this is the case, it is useful to carry out a cost/benefit analysis with clients concerning their stated goals. Here you assess the clients' views of the costs and benefits of their stated goals. Cognitive-behavioural counsellors tend to do this quite formally, using forms to facilitate the process, while counsellors from other traditions may use a similar idea to guide their interventions, but do so with less structure and formality.

2   As noted before, your clients might state their goals, but in reality these goals represent what significant others want them to achieve from counselling. They do not reflect what the clients want from counselling, if anything. I have discussed how to respond to such situations above (see p. 000).

3   Your clients might state goals that they think you want them to achieve from counselling, but these do not reflect their true goals. This is particularly evident in clients who have a dire need for the approval of others. Such people are quite adept at finding out what others want from them and give them what they want. If you suspect that your clients are stating goals that are not their own, but which reflect what they think you want them to achieve, then a good way to respond is to ask them if they would still hold these goals if you wanted them to achieve the opposite. If they would, then their stated goals are probably their own. If not, then their stated goals are not what they want to achieve from counselling but an attempt to please you. This should therefore be the focus for further therapeutic exploration.

Consistent with the flexible view of counselling that underpins this book, my advice to you is to maintain an open mind about your clients' stated goals. Do not assume that they always reflect your clients' true goals nor assume that they always do not. As with other clinical issues, if you are in doubt, discuss the matter with your supervisor.

Overcoming psychological disturbance goals versus promoting self-actualisation goals

When I was training to be a counsellor in the mid-1970s, the distinction between counselling and psychotherapy was sharper than it is now,

Then, the goal of psychotherapy was primarily to help clients overcome psychological disturbance, while the goal of counselling was more to help them promote their personal development. These days, the distinction between counselling and psychotherapy has become blurred, and counsellors have to work both with clients who have problems in the domain of psychological disturbance and with those who are not disturbed, but are not fulfilling their potential in life. The important point to note here is that some clients have psychological problems, but want you to help them fulfil their potential. In truth they are not going to fulfil their potential until they have dealt effectively with their psychological problems. I have found the best way to deal with this situation is to accept the clients' personal development goals, but to help them understand that, before we address these goals, we first need to work towards goals whereby they overcome their psychological problems.

The relationship between your clients' goals and their values

Your clients' goals may be consistent with their values, inconsistent with their values or unrelated to their values. In general, clients are more likely to work towards their goals when these goals are consistent with their values than when they are unrelated to their values, and they are least likely to strive towards their goals when these are inconsistent with their values. For example, consider the case of Ruth. She came to counselling because people were always taking advantage of her. She wanted to address this issue and set as her goal asserting her boundaries with people. One of the values that she held dear in her life was honesty. Since assertion is based on honesty, Ruth persisted in working towards this goal longer than she would have done if honesty had not been an important value to her, and much longer than she would have done if lying to people was valued by her.

My own practice (influenced as it is by CBT) is to encourage clients to make their goals consistent with their values as far as possible (as long as these values are themselves conducive to the clients' long-term well-being) and then to remind themselves of this goal–value link as they work towards their goals.

From a person-centred perspective, counsellors will want to enable clients to identify the distorted, introjected values that they hold and enable them to recognise that they have a choice to retain, modify or reject these values in order to develop a more central locus of evaluation of themselves (Casemore, personal communication).

Your clients may have goals that conflict with one another

When helping clients to set goals for counselling, it is important that you appreciate that such goals may conflict with other goals that your clients might hold. Consider the case of Ralph, who came to counselling for help with his social life. He only had superficial acquaintances and his goal was to deepen his relationships with people. He soon realised that pursuing this goal conflicted with another of his goals, that of being accepted by people. In other words, he saw that if he opened up to people he might deepen his relationships with some, but he might be rejected by others. This resulted in Ralph realising that he had a related problem of fear of rejection which had to be addressed in counselling.

How can you ascertain whether or not your clients have goals that may conflict with their stated goals? My own practice here is to conduct a formal cost–benefit analysis with clients concerning each of their problems and related goals, where I encourage clients to identify the advantages and disadvantages of each problem and associated goal from both a short- and long-term perspective. Reviewing the disadvantages of the goal often reveals other goals that conflict with this target goal. Thus, when I asked Ralph to identify the disadvantages of deepening his relationships with people (his target goal), he responded, 'increases the chances of being rejected'. This revealed the goal of being accepted which potentially conflicted with his goal of deepening his relationships with people.

Thus, when you ask your clients for their goals for counselling, it is important that you take into account that these goals may potentially conflict with their other life goals. Thus you need to assess for this potentiality and intervene accordingly.

When to set goals with your clients

I am often asked when is the best time to set goals with clients. As with many other issues in counselling there is no definitive answer to this question. However, there are a number of rules of thumb that I use in my practice, which I am happy to share with you.

1 It is often important that your clients have the opportunity to express themselves in their own way at the outset before you address the issue of goals.
2 Goals are best set after clients have had the opportunity to talk about their problems *as they see them*.
3 Goals are best set with clients when they are not in a disturbed frame of mind. When they are in this mindset, their elicited goals are often coloured by their disturbed feelings.
4 Goals with respect to psychological disturbance need to be set and pursued before goals that relate to personal development when clients have both.
5 It is important that you realise that clients' goals, once elicited, are not set in stone. They may well change over the course of counselling. Thus, it is important that you periodically review clients' goals during the course of counselling. When your clients' goals do change, it is useful to understand and help them understand the reasons for the shifts in their goals.

Let me now consider goals from the perspective of the counsellor.

Your goals as a counsellor

As I mentioned earlier in the book, Alvin Mahrer (1967) edited an important book in which he asked some of the leading American psychotherapists of the day to discuss their position on the goals of psychotherapy. In his summary of the contributors' views, he argued that the goals of psychotherapy were twofold: (1) to help clients overcome their psychological problems and (2) to promote their personal development. Now, few counsellors would disagree with this analysis, although they would disagree with one another concerning how explicit they should be in helping their clients to articulate their goals. Thus cognitive-behavioural counsellors advocate an explicit emphasis on helping clients to set goals as concretely as possible.

Psychodynamic counsellors are more wary about goal-setting. First, they believe that an emphasis on goals might distract clients whose problems are conflict-based from learning from the process of developing conflictual feelings about their counsellors and from linking these to their past or present conflictual feelings about significant others in their life (Howard, 2010). Secondly, they believe that being goal-oriented may prevent clients whose problems involve deficits from having a positive affective experience in working with their counsellors and developing the ego strength that is derived from such an experience (Howard, 2010). Psychodynamic counsellors also tend to think that goal-setting, particularly at an early stage in counselling, would force clients to specify goals that they have not properly explored or, more importantly, are ambivalent about.

Person-centred counsellors tend to follow their clients on the subject of setting goals and, while they are not against the process, would tend to help clients set goals when this emerges from the clients' frames of reference. They would also help their clients set goals at the level of specificity sought by the clients themselves.

Goals from a working alliance perspective

When we come to consider the issue of goals from a working alliance perspective, one point becomes crystal clear: that it is very important that you and your clients agree on the goals of counselling. Now this agreement does not have to be explicit, as recommended by counsellors in the cognitive-behavioural tradition. It is possible for you and your clients to have *implicit* agreements and work effectively as a team towards these goals. When such agreements are implicit, then the goals are usually implicit as well. Implicit goals are goals that the client indirectly expresses or alludes to rather than makes explicit. While I am not advocating the practice of developing explicit agreements over explicit goals here, since this is not a book on CBT, it is probably the case that there is more scope for lack of agreement over goals that remain implicit than over goals that have been made explicit.

The importance of negotiating goals

If you do work to develop explicit agreements over explicit goals, then it is important for you to recognise that you need to negotiate such goals with your clients. Maluccio (1979) found that counsellors often have more ambitious goals for clients than the clients have for themselves. It is usually counterproductive when you, albeit gently and with the best of intentions, pressure your clients to set goals that are more ambitious than the clients' actual goals. This process can be quite subtle. In particular, clients who believe that they need the approval of significant others may pick up on the idea that you want them to gain certain things from counselling that are more ambitious than those they truly want to achieve. While negotiating goals with clients in general and with this group of clients in particular, it is important that you remain as neutral as possible, so that you don't influence their goal-setting. If necessary, ask clients if their goals would be the same if you would take issue with their goals and in fact advocate the opposite. If they can maintain their goals in the face of your hypothesised, and others' real, opposition, then these goals are likely to be genuine.

Responding to clients' initially stated goals

So far I have spoken about eliciting your clients' goals. This is not the end of the story because when your clients first disclose their goals these may be seen to be problematic for a number of reasons (some of which I discussed earlier in this chapter). Table 4.1 lists problematic goals and possible counsellor responses.

Table 4.1 Problematic goals, suggested counsellor responses and reformulated goals.

Problematic goal	Suggested counsellor response	Reformulated goal
A goal that specifies a change in other people (e.g. 'I want my husband to be more understanding towards me').	A goal that specifies a change in other people (e.g. 'I want my husband to be more understanding towards me').	...A goal that specifies a change in the client's own behaviour which may influence the other person to act in the desired manner (e.g. I want to show more understanding of my husband and see what effect doing so has on his behaviour).
A goal that is unrealistic and unachievable (e.g. 'I never want to feel anxiety again').	Point out why the client's goal is unrealistic and unachievable, often because it is perfectionistic and help them to set ...	... A goal that is achievable, realistic and non-perfectionistic (e.g. 'I want to minimise my anxiety and learn how to deal with it constructively when I feel threatened').
A goal that you suspect has been set *for* the client rather than *by* the client (e.g. 'My wife wants me to learn to control my temper').	Encourage the client, if necessary, to imagine that the other person is leaving the goals of counselling completely up to the client. Then ask the client to set ...	... A goal that is achievable, realistic and non-perfectionistic (e.g. 'I want to minimise my anxiety and learn how to deal with it constructively when I feel threatened').
A goal that specifies the absence of something rather than the presence of something (e.g. 'I want to stop losing my temper when my employees turn up late for work').	Point out that it is much easier to work towards achieving the presence of something rather than the absence of something. Then ask the client to set ...	... A goal that specifies the presence of a desired state (e.g. 'I want to communicate my annoyance and assert myself by letting my employees know what the consequences will be if they turn up late for work').

(Continued)

Table 4.1 *(Continued)*

Problematic goal	Suggested counsellor response	Reformulated goal
A goal that is so vague that it is meaningless (e.g. 'I want to live ethically').	Help the client to see that you don't understand what the vague goal means. If they cannot specify this, suggest that you need to explore with hem the meaning of the opposite to he vague goal (e.g. 'What does living ethically mean to you?'). Otherwise, ask the client to specify as far as they can the specific referents of the goal (e.g. 'If you were living ethically what would you be doing that you are not doing now?' As a result ...	... The goal should be a clear and specific representation of the vague expression first made (e.g. 'I want to give honest answers when family members ask me about my feelings').
A goal that is clearly based on disturbed feelings (e.g. a client with anxiety problems who says, 'I want to put off working off on my project until I feel ready to do it').	Help your client to see that their goal is an expression of her emotional problem rather than a solution to it. Then ask the client to set ...	... A goal that targets the disturbed emotion (e.g. 'I want to deal with my anxiety about my project and approach the task rather than avoid it').
A goal that is based on personal development, when the client has a psychological problem (e.g. a depressed client who says 'I want to give up my safe job and do something I have always wanted to do: set up my own business').	Help your client to see that the best time to set a personal development goal is when she is free from psychological disturbance. Then ask the client to set ...	... A goal that targets the disturbed emotion (e.g. 'I want to deal with my depression before considering whether or not now is a good time to risk giving up my safe job and embark on an exciting, but uncertain enterprise').

When you respond to your clients' problematic goals you are initiating a process of negotiating goals with these clients in order to select a goal to which you both can commit. The term 'negotiation' means that both your own and your client's goal-related concerns are taken seriously and a compromise is reached when the client's initially stated goal is problematic. How this negotiation is done (and indeed, if it is done at all) depends on your theoretical orientation.

Even when you and your clients are in agreement concerning their goals, the clients may wish to modify their goals when they appreciate the effort needed to achieve these goals. Knowing this, your clients may wish to modify their goals to those that are less ambitious, but more in line with the effort they are prepared to make in order to achieve the goals.

As a consequence, from a working alliance perspective, as a counsellor you increase the chances of helping clients to reach their goals when you both agree to pursue goals that are:

- within your clients' direct control to achieve;
- realistic and achievable;
- set by your clients themselves;
- positively stated;
- clearly stated;
- uncontaminated by psychological disturbance;
- based on the present state of clients (an overcoming-disturbance goal when clients are disturbed; a personal development goal when they are not);
- set to reflect the amount of effort clients are prepared to make to achieve the goals.

The importance of renegotiating goals

Once you have agreed goals with your clients, it is tempting to think that the matter is now closed and you can concentrate on helping your clients to work towards achieving their objectives. Actually, this is not the case, as your clients' goals can change over the course of counselling.

Clients' goals may change for a variety of reasons. Here is a sample of such reasons:

1   Clients' goals may change in response to the work you have done with them in the consulting room. Thus, they may realise that the goals they set at the outset were too ambitious, not ambitious enough, or based on values they have explored and come to reject. For example, it is fairly common for clients to appreciate during the course of counselling that acquiring material things is not fulfilling, and family and spiritual values are more important to them than they had realised. Reviewing their goals at such a juncture usually leads them to set new goals in line with the newly prized values.

2   When clients do not make expected progress towards their goals, this may be due to a variety of factors. First, they may have been ambivalent about the goals which they initially agreed with you. They may even have been implicitly opposed to these goals, but could find no way of expressing this. When lack of progress towards goals occurs then you should explore the reasons for it, intervene accordingly and renegotiate goals when necessary.

3   Sometimes life events take place which make your clients' goals redundant. Consider the case of Stuart, whose agreed goal for counselling was to deal with his destructive envious feelings towards his colleagues at work. Then his wife was diagnosed as having breast cancer to which he responded with severe anxiety. His envious feelings did not seem as important any more and we renegotiated the goal of dealing with his anxiety about his wife's illness.

For these and other reasons it is important to keep in mind that you may have to renegotiate your clients' goals on one or more occasions over the course of counselling. However, when your clients' goals are stable then you can get down to the business of helping them work towards them.

The impact of context on counselling goals

So far in this book, I have considered the impact of the context in which counselling is practised on that practice in two ways. First, I have compared agencies that have a policy of time-constrained counselling with those that don't set such constraints and second, I have considered the influence of the focus of the agency (e.g. spiritual vs. medical) on the work of the counsellor. Let me now discuss these two variables with respect to their influence on goal-setting in counselling

The context of time and goals

In counselling agencies, where time-limited counselling is the norm and where specific goal-setting occurs, the effect of such time constraints are that counsellors negotiate goals with their clients that are focused on one or two specific problems. The goals negotiated also tend to be specific in nature. The main advantage of time constraints in this domain of the alliance is that it does encourage both counsellors and clients to be goal focused. The main disadvantage is that the goals tend to be unambitious in nature. The emphasis is much more on helping clients to get back to where they were before they experienced their problems rather than on taking them on to a more advanced stage of psychological development.

In counselling agencies, where such time constraints are not the norm, then the main advantage of goals that are set is that they can be quite ambitious and meaningful for the client's long-term development. The main disadvantage of such open-ended work is that it may lead to counselling that is directionless with respect to client goals and outcome.

The context of focus and goals

Many counselling agencies have either an explicit or an implicit focus which frames its work. Thus, some agencies have a religious focus, while others have a non-religious focus. Some are focused on medical problems while others are focused on work problems. Particularly where resources are limited with an understandable knock-on effect on how much time can be offered to clients, there tends to be a corresponding emphasis on setting goals that reflect the focus of the agency concerned. Thus, consider the case of Eric. He was referred to a counselling agency who had a contract with Eric's employers to offer time-limited, work-based counselling to its employees. He had a conflictual relationship with his boss and also problems at home dealing with his teenage daughter. Eric wanted to be helped to deal with his boss more assertively and to understand how to communicate with his daughter. Having established that the second problem was not related to his work problem, Eric's counsellor explained to Eric that it was outside her brief to help him with his problems with his daughter as she was engaged only to deal with work issues. Ideally, counselling should adopt a whole person focus. Practically, its focus is often more limited as the example of Eric shows.

The work that you and your clients do in the service of their goals is referred to as 'tasks' in the working alliance literature and this component of the working alliance is the subject of the following chapter.

Discussion issues

1   What is your stance on goal-setting in counselling?
2   How do you respond when your clients want to achieve unrealistic goals?
3   How do you respond when your clients' goals conflict with one another?
4   If you do set goals with your clients, when do you do so?
5   What impact does the context in which you work as a counsellor have on the goals that you set with your clients?

FIVE

Tasks

The fourth component in my reconceptualisation of Bordin's (1979) working alliance model is tasks – activities carried out by you and your clients which are goal-directed in nature. The other books in this series present specific approaches to counselling where a predominant feature of each approach is its specification of the tasks that both counsellor and client are required to carry out in the service of meeting the latter's goals. Such tasks may be broad in nature (for example, to engage in the task of self-exploration in person-centred counselling) or more specific (to engage in Socratic dialogue in cognitive therapy).

However, when an alliance perspective on tasks is taken, the slant is different from one which emphasises the content of such tasks, and several questions become salient. The following is a sample of such questions since a comprehensive discussion of tasks from a working alliance perspective would again merit a whole book.

1. Do your clients understand that they have therapeutic tasks to perform and do they know the nature of these tasks?

If your clients do not either explicitly or implicitly understand (a) that they have tasks to perform in the counselling process and (b) what these tasks are, then a potential obstacle to their progress through the counselling process is present. As with other potential obstacles this may be dealt with by referring the matter for discussion to that part of the counselling dialogue that I call 'the reflection process' where you and your client step back and discuss what has gone on between you during counselling sessions. Aware of how important it is for clients to understand their role in the counselling process and, more specifically, what their tasks are in that process, some counsellors formally attempt to initiate clients into their role at the outset of the process (see Orne and Wender, 1968).

2. If your clients understand the nature of the tasks that they are called upon to execute can they see that performing the tasks will help them to achieve their goals?

From a working alliance perspective, tasks are best conceptualised as ways of achieving therapeutic goals. Thus, your clients may understand what their tasks are, but they may be uncertain how carrying these out may help them to achieve their goals. For example, a client may wish to handle interpersonal conflict in a more constructive way, e.g. by being assertive with his spouse rather than aggressive. However, he may not see the link between being able to do this and being asked to free associate in the relatively unstructured setting of psychodynamic counselling. Alternatively, another client may not see how disputing her irrational beliefs about competence (as required in Rational Emotive Behaviour Therapy) will necessarily help her to be productively aroused rather than anxious in examinations. Thus, from an alliance perspective it is very important that you help your clients to understand the link between carrying out their counselling tasks and achieving their goals. This holds true whether the clients' tasks are to be performed within the counselling session or between counselling sessions in their everyday lives.

3. Do your clients believe that they have to work to change?

Counselling and psychotherapy tend to have an aura of mystery about them, compounded by those practitioners who are reluctant to be explicit about what they do and what they expect clients to do in counselling. This vagueness about the counselling process does nothing to dispel the idea in some clients' minds that all they have to do in counselling is to turn up and talk. In practice, for counselling to be effective your clients have to engage in some 'work'. What this work consists of depends on the nature of the clients' problems and the therapeutic orientation of their counsellors. Unless clients accept and implement the principle of 'working for change', then the gains that they are likely to achieve from counselling may be superficial and ephemeral. It follows from this that you should encourage your clients to adopt and implement a 'work to change' philosophy if you are going to be truly helpful to them.

4. Do your clients have the capability to carry out the therapeutic tasks required of them?

In order to engage in counselling tasks, clients do need to be able to perform these tasks. Thus, not all clients will have the capability to engage in Socratic questioning in cognitive therapy or REBT. Not having the capability to engage in certain counselling tasks means that no amount of training to use these tasks will help. This is in sharp contrast to situations when your clients may have the capability, but not the necessary *skills* to perform these tasks, in which case they will benefit from some training and/or instructions concerning the necessary skills and how to use them.

Sometimes it is relatively easy to determine that clients do not have the capability to engage in certain counselling tasks. Thus, a task may require a relatively high level of intellectual intelligence, and it is clear to you that a particular client just does not have this. However, in the majority of cases, it is less clear whether or not clients have the required capability. In such cases, the best way of determining this is trial and error. If, after a reasonable number of attempts to encourage a client to use a particular task and after appropriate training in task-relevant skills, the client still cannot engage in the task, then it is reasonable to conclude that the client does not have the necessary task-related capability. Skilled counsellors are able to determine this without demoralising their client because they have helped these clients to see that one of their tasks as counsellors is to identify appropriate tasks for their clients, a procedure which involves trial and error. They also stress that clients bring to counselling different capabilities, and that effective counselling involves matching counselling tasks to particular client capabilities. If one of your clients becomes disturbed about their lack of a relevant capability when you have taken appropriate steps to minimise such distress, their reaction is likely to reflect one of their problems and should be put on the therapeutic agenda.

5. Do your clients have the necessary skills to carry out the therapeutic tasks required of them?

As I mentioned above, skills are different from capabilities in that clients may be capable of engaging in a process of examining their dysfunctional beliefs, for example, but may not know how to do this. Once they are taught these skills then they are able to give expression to their capability. So although the execution of particular tasks may facilitate client change, if your clients do not have the necessary skills in their repertoire to carry these out, then this poses a threat to the working alliance in the task domain.

It may be productive, therefore, for clients to receive specific training in executing their tasks if they lack the skills to do so at a given point. For example, the client task of disputing irrational beliefs in REBT involves the following skills:

- becoming aware of feeling emotionally disturbed and/or of acting in a self-defeating manner;
- identifying one or more irrational beliefs that underpin such disturbance;
- questioning the irrationality implicit in such beliefs;
- convincingly answering one's own questions; and
- constructing rational alternatives to these irrational beliefs.

It should be clear from such a detailed analysis of client task behaviour that the client's ability to execute such a task successfully depends upon (a) how effective the counsellor has been in training the client to do this within the counselling sessions and (b) how much successful practice the client has engaged in both within and between counselling sessions.

6. Do your clients have the confidence to execute the relevant tasks?

A similar point can be made here as has been made above. Certain client tasks (and in particular those that clients are asked to do between sessions – the so-called 'homework assignments') require a certain degree of task confidence on the part of clients if they are to execute them successfully. So your clients may understand the nature of the task, see its therapeutic relevance, have the ability and the skills to carry it out, but may still not do so because they predict that they don't have the confidence. If this is the case then you can prepare your clients in one of two ways. First, you may need to help the clients practise the tasks in controlled conditions (usually within the counselling session) to the extent that that they feel confident to do the said tasks on their own. Secondly, you may encourage your clients to carry out the tasks unconfidently, pointing out that confidence comes from the result of undertaking an activity (that is, from practice) and is rarely experienced before the activity is first attempted. Counsellors who use analogies within the experience of the clients themselves (for example, learning to drive a car) often succeed at helping them understand this important point.

7. Does the task have sufficient therapeutic potency to facilitate goal achievement?

If all the aforementioned conditions are met (that is, clients understand the nature and therapeutic relevance of task execution, and they have sufficient ability skills and confidence to perform the relevant tasks), your clients may still not gain therapeutic benefit from undertaking the tasks because these tasks may not have sufficient therapeutic potency to help them achieve their goals. For example, certain client tasks, if sufficiently well carried out, will probably lead to client change. Thus exposing oneself, in vivo (i.e. in reality) or through imagination, to a phobic object will likely yield some therapeutic benefit (Rachman and Wilson, 1980). However, certain tasks may have much less therapeutic potency to achieve a similar result. For example, it has yet to be demonstrated that free association or disputing one's irrational beliefs in the counselling session rather than in the feared situation have much therapeutic effect in overcoming phobias. Here, then, your task as counsellor is to become au fait with the current research literature on the subject at hand and not discourage your clients by asking them to carry out tasks which are unlikely, even under the most favourable conditions, to produce much therapeutic benefit.

In this respect there are certain client problems which do seem to call for the execution of specific client tasks. Apart from phobic problems mentioned above, obsessive-compulsive problems seem to call for the client to employ some variant of response prevention in their everyday lives (Rachman and Wilson, 1980) and problems of depression seem to call for the client to modify distorted thought patterns (Beck et al., 1979) and troublesome elements of their significant interpersonal relationships (Klerman et al., 1984) in order to gain therapeutic benefit. In Britain, the National Institute of Clinical Excellence (NICE) publishes up-to-date guidelines outlining which therapies are likely to be effective for a range of client problems, although for the most part performing a wide variety of tasks may yield a comparable therapeutic result (Stiles et al., 1986).

8. Do the tasks that you execute and/or that your clients execute serve to perpetuate their problems?

It is important to bear in mind that what you do in counselling and what your clients do both in counselling and outside counselling may serve unwittingly to perpetuate their problems rather than help them deal effectively with these problems. First, your clients may, at their own suggestion, do various things which, while being designed to help them overcome their problems, have the opposite effect. Thus, many anxious clients seek to avoid anxiety-provoking situations before they get anxious, or withdraw from these situations when they get anxious, in an attempt to deal with these anxious feelings. Such behaviour prevents clients from facing their fears and dealing appropriately with them and thus they remain anxious in the long run.

Some counsellors respond to their clients' anxieties with inappropriate reassurance and suggestions that their clients distract themselves when they feel anxious. In the first case, reassurance is often ineffective because when clients are anxious they are often not reassurable and, in the second case, distraction is a form of withdrawal and as a result clients again do not face their fears armed appropriately with coping strategies.

9. Do your clients understand the nature of your tasks as counsellor and how these relate to their own tasks and to their goals?

So far I have focused on issues which deal with your clients' tasks. However, in addition to the foregoing, it is important that your clients your interventions and their rationale understand (either at an explicit or an implicit level). In particular, the more clients can understand how their tasks relate to your tasks as counsellor, the more each of you can concentrate on effective task execution, the purpose of which, as has been stressed above, is to facilitate the attainment of clients' goals. Should your clients be puzzled about your tasks and how these relate to their own, they will be sidetracked from performing their own tasks and begin to question what you are doing and perhaps even your competence as a counsellor. These doubts, if not explored and dealt with in the reflection process, constitute a threat at all levels of the working alliance. An additional strategy that may prevent the development of your clients' doubts is for you as counsellor to explain, at an appropriate stage in the counselling process, your tasks and why you are intervening in the way you have chosen to. As you do this you will maximise the impact of such explanations if you can show your clients how your tasks complement theirs and how both sets of tasks relate to the attainment of your clients' goals.

10. Are your clients in a sufficiently good frame of mind to execute their tasks?

So far I have outlined some of the favourable conditions that need to exist in counselling if your clients are to get the most out of counselling in the task domain. No matter how favourable these conditions are, your clients need to be in a sufficiently good frame of mind to capitalise on them. If your clients are very anxious, for example, then they will probably not be able to implement tasks that involve a lot of focused attention. And if clients are very depressed then they may not be able to engage in very active therapeutic tasks. In such cases it is important that you do not ask clients to engage in counselling tasks that are too much for them at that point in time. To do so would be to discourage them. Continually monitor your clients' frame of mind and encourage them to engage in tasks that are challenging but not overwhelming for them at any given point in time (Dryden, 1985). Conversely asking clients to engage in tasks that are insufficiently challenging for them may also deprive them of the opportunity of getting the most out of counselling. If clients can easily do something then the therapeutic value of such tasks may be minimal.

Tasks and your expertise as a counsellor

How much of the effectiveness of counselling is dependent on your expertise as a counsellor? Quite a bit, research shows (Beutler et al., 2004). Here is a sample of issues that pertain to your expertise in executing your tasks.

Counsellor skill

Studies on counsellors' skill in executing their tasks in the therapeutic process (for example, Luborsky et al., 1985) have brought to light an important and quite obvious point that the skill with which counsellors perform their own tasks in therapy has a positive influence on client outcome. From an alliance perspective, the degree to which clients make progress may be due in some measure to the skill with which counsellors perform their tasks. The implications for the training and supervision of counsellors are that trainers and supervisors should seek concrete and detailed evidence of how skilfully counsellors execute their tasks, and should rely less upon counsellors' descriptions of what they did in counselling sessions and more on specific ways of appraising skill (for example, through digital voice recordings of counselling sessions, or at the very least through very detailed process notes).

If you are skilful in the execution of your tasks, you increase the chances that your clients will have confidence in your ability and see you as being helpful (Pinsof and Catherall, 1986). However, it is important that you realise that you develop skill as a therapist gradually and that if you want to be competent as a practitioner you need to accept moving from a state of conscious incompetence to conscious competence and hence to unconscious competence.

Explaining one's counselling approach and gaining informed consent

I mentioned earlier in this book (see Chapter 3) that from a working alliance perspective it is important that your clients understand your therapeutic approach so that they can give their informed consent before proceeding with treatment. Not only is gaining clients' informed consent an ethical position, it is also good practice to do so. For giving informed consent indicates that clients understand your therapeutic approach and are actively choosing to involve themselves in the counselling process. These are both therapeutic factors associated with good therapeutic outcome.

It follows from this that two core skills that you need to develop to a high level of competence are (1) explaining your therapeutic approach to a variety of different clients and (2) gaining informed consent. Both of these skills involve your eliciting and dealing with your clients' doubts, reservations and objections to your therapeutic approach and correcting any misconceptions that they reveal in the process. During training you can practise these skills with your fellow trainees, make digital voice recordings of these sessions and play them to your trainer and fellow trainees for feedback on how to improve your skills in these two areas.

Making judicious referrals

It is important to appreciate that not everyone who seeks your help will be suitable for that help. This may be the case for a number of reasons.

First, they may actually be looking for a different type of help. For example, some people come for counselling for advice with their practical problems. They think that the word 'counselling' means advice, a misconception often promulgated by the popular media.

Secondly, clients may be suitable for counselling but are seeking a different type of approach from the one you are offering. For example, many years ago when I worked in Birmingham, a man rang me and asked me if I practised an approach to therapy known as RT. As you know I practise Rational Emotive Behaviour Therapy (REBT), but it was originally known as rational therapy (RT) and I thought that the man was referring to REBT but in its earliest form. On that basis, I agreed to see him. However it soon transpired that he was seeking Reichian therapy (RT), a body-work oriented therapy, very different from REBT!

Thirdly, your clients may be seeking counselling, may be suitable for the approach to counselling that you practise, but you may not be the best person to see him or her. Thus, your clients may be better helped by counsellors of the same gender as themselves but different from yours, or they may be better helped by someone who has a different personality type from you. Furthermore, your clients may be seeking help for a problem which requires specialist skills that you do not have, but you know a colleague who does.

It follows from the above that determining the best type of help for the people who have come to see you and making a judicious referral if necessary are core skills that you need to develop. It is particularly important when you make a referral that you inspire clients with the hope that the person to whom you are referring them is the best person that you know who can offer the most appropriate help.

Varying the use of your tasks

A theme that has run through this chapter so far, albeit implicitly, is that since clients vary (along several key dimensions), counsellors need to vary accordingly their own contribution to the counselling process. This has clear implications for client goals since there is more than one way 'to skin a therapeutic cat', and if one set of counsellor tasks is not helpful to particular clients then others may be. It also has implications for counselling bonds. For example, Hutchins (1984) has argued that counsellors can improve the relationship they have with their clients by varying the tasks they use with different clients. While he focuses on the client's predominant modes of dealing with the world, he makes the point that counsellors too have similar predominant modes.

While in an ideal world effective counsellors would, with equal facility, be able to use cognitive, behavioural and affective tasks, the fact that counsellors have their own limitations means that it is a temptation for counsellors to restrict themselves to using tasks which reflect their predominant orientation (cognitive, emotive or behavioural). Hutchins's analysis implies that should counsellors restrict themselves to using particular intervention modes (that is, cognitive, emotive or behavioural), they would help a smaller range of clients than if they became more flexible in freely and appropriately using cognitive, emotive and behavioural tasks.

It follows from this that to increase their effectiveness in the task domain of the alliance, counsellors need to acknowledge their own task preferences and work on broadening their own range of task behaviour – a task which itself calls for continual exposure to what therapeutic models other than their own preferred model have to offer. This would mean that counsellors of different orientations would learn from each other to a greater extent than is currently the case, a point grasped by the movement exploring eclecticism and integration in counselling and psychotherapy which is now firmly established on both sides of the Atlantic.

If counsellors do not adopt the challenge of broadening their task-related repertoire then what they need to do, as discussed above, is to refer clients who are likely to benefit from different counselling approaches to practitioners of these approaches. To assume that one's own approach will help everyone is a misguided 'one-size-fits-all' viewpoint that open-minded practitioners tend not to hold.

Capitalising on the client's learning style and preferred modalities

As used here, counselling tasks (broadly conceptualised) are the means by which clients achieve their goals. If clients do achieve their goals it is because they have learned something new (for example, to see things differently and/or to act differently).

When you take a working alliance perspective on client learning, you need to consider how best to facilitate learning for each of your clients. For example, you need to discover how each of your clients best learns and you must then capitalise on this by tailoring your interventions accordingly.

Let me illustrate this by discussing two clients who had similar problems, but different learning styles. Rita and Kathy both experienced anxiety about public speaking and avoided it whenever they could. They were both worried that they would say something foolish while speaking formally in public. Rita learned best by finding out how other people had overcome similar fears and applying what made sense to her from their experiences. Kathy, on the other hand, said that it was important to her to discover the possible origins of her fear before learning how to deal with it. I encouraged Rita to surf the Net and develop a portfolio of how others had successfully dealt with this fear. I also arranged for her to meet some of my former clients who had learned how to speak in public without anxiety. As a result of these experiences, I encouraged Rita to put together a way of tackling the problem that was right for her.

With Kathy, I took a very different tack. I helped her to review her past experiences of speaking in public and she discovered that it started after her father had joked about how squeaky her voice sounded when he had heard her speak in a school play when she was ten years of age. I helped her to understand the dysfunctional beliefs she had formed as a result of this experience and was still unwittingly perpetuating by avoiding public speaking. For Kathy, practising healthy alternatives to these dysfunctional beliefs while revisiting in imagination that early experience was an important precursor to practising those beliefs in the present. By contrast, I never discussed the possible historical roots of Rita's problem because she did not mention this as an important ingredient of her learning style.

My friend and colleague Dr Arnold Lazarus (1989) has cogently argued that there are seven modalities of human experience that need to be considered when working with clients: Behaviour, Affect (or Emotions), Sensation, Imagery, Cognition (or Thinking), Interpersonal

Relationships and Physiological Functioning. These seven modalities are known by the acronym BASIC ID (the D stands for drugs, the most common way of dealing with problems in the physiological functioning modality). Lazarus argues that people vary according to the modalities that they typically use and that it is useful to develop a person's modality profile by asking them to rate themselves on a 0–10 scale indicating varying degree of modality use.

Let me show how this informed my work with two clients experiencing a similar anger problem. Bill scored highly in the behavioural, interpersonal and sensation modalities. I helped Bill use these modalities particularly when he first noticed himself getting angry by encouraging him to use a sensory (in this case, olfactory) cue to relax (his aftershave), before capitalising on his strong tendency to use the behavioural and interpersonal modalities: I encouraged him to use his assertive skills with the person with whom he was angry. Neville, on the other hand, scored high on the cognitive and imagery modalities, but low on the behavioural and interpersonal modalities. Therefore I taught Neville cognitive restructuring techniques to deal with provocations before encouraging him to see himself asserting himself with the person with whom he was angry. I then encouraged him to use assertion in real life. Since, in general, people require more help in using tasks in their non-preferred modalities, I spent more time in counselling on teaching Neville how to assert himself in real life than I did with Bill.

From the above it is clear that it is useful to know your clients' modality strengths in developing a jointly agreed treatment plan. But sometimes you will need to help clients to become more proficient in modalities in which they are less proficient. For example, very passive clients often need to learn to be more active in the behavioural modality. A full discussion about when to capitalise on a client's pre-existing modality strengths and when to encourage them to learn to develop greater competence in non-preferred modalities is an advanced topic beyond the introductory scope of the present book. For more information on using modalities to inform counselling practice, consult Lazarus (1985, 1989).

Helping your clients to get the most out of their tasks

Given the fact that your clients do have tasks to carry out in counselling, however specifically or broadly you conceive these tasks, should you do anything as a counsellor to get the most out of these tasks? Working alliance theory would argue that you should, otherwise you leave to chance whether or not your clients will do all they can to help themselves. So how can you help them to get the most out of their tasks? Here is a selection of possible interventions:

1 Explain clearly to your clients what their tasks are and answer any questions they have about these tasks.
2 Help your clients see clearly the relationship between their tasks and their goals. Encourage them to keep this connection clearly in mind during counselling.
3 Modify these tasks after taking into account your clients' strengths and weaknesses. You can do this before clients carry out their tasks and after they have done so. In the latter case, you can suggest modifications to the tasks based on your clients' feedback of their attempts to use them.
4 Train your clients in these tasks if relevant (see Dryden, 2004, for an example of training clients to become proficient in REBT client skills).
5 Problem solve any obstacles to client task execution.
6 Have alternative client tasks in mind if your clients refuse to or cannot carry out their original tasks.
7 If you negotiate homework assignments with your clients, make sure that your clients specify what they are going to do, when they are going to do it and how often. Problem-solve possible obstacles to homework completion.

Encouraging clients to get the most out of their tasks is easier to conceive if you are a counsellor practising an approach where clients' tasks are more specific in nature (for example CBT). However, the issue is relevant if you are a person-centred or psychodynamic counsellor, in which case I suggest that you discuss how you might approach this with your trainer and/or supervisor.

Using tasks at different stages of change

In the final chapter of this book I will consider the process of counselling from a working alliance perspective and show how each of the four components of the working alliance changes over the course of counselling. But here I want to make the point that both your tasks as counsellor and your clients' tasks change during counselling. For example, in REBT, the counsellor's and client's tasks change over the course of counselling as follows.

Counsellors' tasks in REBT

I have organised the tasks that REBT counsellors are called upon to carry out according to the phase of counselling in which such tasks are most salient. Please bear in mind that this does not mean that these tasks are not used by these counsellors in the other phases.

The beginning phase

- Establish a therapeutic alliance.
- Socialise the client into REBT.
- Begin to assess and intervene on target problem.
- Teach the ABCs of REBT.
- Deal with your client's doubts.

The middle phase

- Follow through on target problem.
- Encourage your client to engage in relevant tasks.
- Work on client's other problems.
- Identify and challenge core irrational beliefs.
- Deal with obstacles to change.
- Encourage your client to maintain and enhance gains.
- Undertake relapse prevention and deal with vulnerability factors.
- Encourage your client to become his or her own counsellor.

The ending phase

- Decide on when and how to end.
- Encourage your client to summarise what has been learned.
- Attribute improvement to client's efforts.
- Deal with obstacles to ending.
- Agree on criteria for follow-ups and for resuming therapy.

Clients' tasks in REBT

I have organised the tasks that clients are called upon to carry out in REBT in the following way. The tasks at the top reflect tasks that are more salient at the beginning. Further down the list are the tasks that are more salient later in the process. Once again, please bear in mind that this does not mean that tasks listed at the top are not relevant later on in the process, and to some degree vice versa.

Specify problems

- Be open to the REBT framework.
- Apply the specific principle of emotional responsibility.
- Apply the principle of therapeutic responsibility,
- Disclose doubts, difficulties and blocks to change.
- Identify and deal with obstacles to change.
- Generalise learning.
- Undertake relapse prevention and deal with vulnerability factors.
- Take responsibility for becoming their own counsellor.
- Seek counselling help in the future when self-help fails.

The context of counselling and its impact on counselling tasks

Throughout this book, I have considered the impact of the context in which counselling is practised on that practice. The main impact of context on tasks comes about through the orientation propounded by the counselling agency. Thus, if an agency is based on psychodynamic counselling then this orientation will obviously influence the tasks carried out by its counsellors. Aside from this obvious point and taking a working alliance stance, my view is that the influence of the context on counselling tasks is mainly through the impact that it has on bonds, views and goals. For example, the counsellor's tasks are influenced by:

- the depth of relationship that can be developed with the client;
- the type of goals that can be negotiated with the client;
- the views that are taken of client problems and their 'treatment';

The amount of time that the counsellor can spend with the client is often the main determinant here and as argued above has its effect on counselling tasks through the impact on the other domains of the working alliance.

Having discussed briefly the changes that occur over time in the task domain of the working alliance before the above section on context, I want to end this book on counselling in a nutshell by considering the process of counselling from beginning to end from a working alliance perspective.

Discussion issues

1 How do you conceptualise the tasks that you perform as a counsellor?
2 What tasks do your clients need to perform in counselling?
3 What do you think of the view that clients can be trained to perform their tasks more effectively in counselling?
4 Under what conditions might you vary your task behaviour in counselling?
5 What impact does the context in which you work as a counsellor have on your counselling tasks?

SIX

Counselling as a Process

In this final chapter, I am going to consider the process of counselling from the perspective of working alliance theory. While it is traditional to discuss the process of counselling in terms of its beginning, middle and end phases, I am going to approach this subject a little differently. I will discuss the process of counselling in terms of a number of sequential stages and show how working alliance theory informs the work of counselling at each stage. In doing so, I will draw on the work of Egan (2002) and Beitman (1987), who have both outlined a stage-based model of counselling, and on the work of Prochaska et al. (1994) who have outlined a stages-of-change model which helps counsellors understand which stage of change a particular client is in on a particular issue. Of all the chapters of this book, this is the one which is the most personal in that the model that I have developed here has been shaped by ideas with which I have particularly resonated. I make no apology in presenting this model despite its personal bias.

Dryden's stage-based model of the counselling process

My stage-based model of the counselling process has six stages.[1] I will briefly outline them before going on to discuss them more fully, one at

---

[1] There other process views in the literature, most notable being the one developed by Rogers (1961) who outlined seven stages of the process of counselling.

a time. As I do so, I will emphasise how working alliance theory can influence your work at each stage.

Briefly, the six stages in my model are as follows:

1   Engagement
2   Exploration
3   Cognitive-Experiential Understanding
4   Change based on Cognitive-Experiential Understanding
5   Working Through
6   Ending

Engagement

As I mentioned in Chapter 3, when someone first contacts you for help, it is useful to assume that they are in the applicant role rather than the client role. An applicant is someone who is considering a number of issues (to be discussed below). In saying this, I am not asserting that they are actively considering these issues in a conscious way, although of course this may be the case with some people with respect to some of these issues. I am saying that these are the issues that are often being implicitly considered by your potential clients, and if some clients do not come back after their initial contact with you it is because they are not satisfied on one or more of the following issues.

Is the help that the counsellor has to offer me, the help that I need?

This issue can be said to be related to the views, goals and tasks domains of the working alliance. Thus, clients need to have an under-standing of how you work (*views*), have a sense of what this implies for what both you and they are going to do in counselling (*tasks*), and understand how all this is going to help them in the ways that they want to be helped (*goals*).

This means that one of your initial *tasks* as a counsellor is to explain what you have to offer your potential clients so that they can make an informed decision concerning whether or not they may find helpful what you have to offer.

Am I going to get along with the counsellor and is s/he the best person to help me?

These two issues centre on the *bond* domain of the working alliance. At the very first point of contact with you, a potential client is gauging how you respond to them. This means that you need to pay attention to how you speak to potential clients on the phone and how you greet them when you first meet them. This issue also applies to how other people with whom you work (for example, receptionists) respond to the initial contacts of potential clients. I once worked in a counselling service which had a high percentage of clients who had booked appointments failing to keep these appointments. An investigation revealed that two of the receptionists were perceived as unwelcoming and having an abrupt telephone manner, and this accounted for this early drop-out phenomenon.

Thus, potential clients want to know if they can get on with you and if you are going to offer them a professional service, and it is your initial task as a counsellor to attend to these *bond* components of the alliance.

Prochaska et al.'s (1994) stages-of-change model of counselling (developed in work with substance-misuse problems, but more widely applicable) notes that people coming for counselling may be in a pre-contemplative stage of change. This means that they may not regard themselves as having problems which need counselling help, but they arrive at your office because other people (most often family members, friends or employers) or agencies (most frequently the courts) have insisted that they seek help for problems that are obvious to these other people and agencies, but not acknowledged by the person being pressed to seek help. While a full discussion of how to engage this group of 'reluctant' clients lies outside the scope of this book, you might like to consult the literature on an intervention known as motivational interviewing (for example, Miller and Rollnick, 2002) which is increasingly being used with such 'clients'.

Once a person has made an informed decision to proceed based on their initial judgement that you can be helpful to them and that they feel comfortable enough to work with you, they can be said to become your client and you can proceed to explore their concerns.

Exploration

One of your early *tasks* as a counsellor is to create a climate in which your clients feel free enough to disclose to you why they have sought counselling at this point in their lives. Creating this climate of safety can best be seen as facilitating work in the *bond* domain of the working alliance. Once your clients feel free to disclose their concerns you can begin to help them to explore these concerns. Encouraging them to talk in their own way and communicating empathic understanding of what they saying are crucial tasks at this stage of the counselling process. Research has shown that counsellor empathy encourages clients to explore their problems at a core level (Beutler et al., 2004), but it is important that this exploration be paced so that your client feels safe to engage in this exploration, rather than feel threatened by the engagement.

While psychodynamic and person-centred counsellors engage their clients in an open exploration of their clients' concerns, cognitive-behavioural counsellors, after an initial open-ended exploratory phase, help their clients to explore their problems in a more structured way using, for example, an ABC framework, in which A stands for an event, B for the thoughts and beliefs that are held about the event, and C for the emotional and behavioural consequences of the thoughts and beliefs at B.

During this period of exploration, clients continue to ask themselves, albeit implicitly, a number of questions. I will discuss three here.

Does the counsellor understand me?

Egan (2002), among others, has written about 'accurate' empathy. This term reflects not only your attempts to understand your clients from their frame of reference, but how accurate you are in doing so. While most clients will not expect you to be accurate in all of your attempts to understand them, they will conclude that you are not sufficiently understanding of their concerns if you frequently fail to understand them from their point of view. If this happens, your client may well terminate counselling at this early stage.

Do I feel comfortable exploring my concerns with the counsellor?

During the exploration phase your clients will get a sense of how comfortable they are in exploring their concerns with you. If they are not sufficiently comfortable they may well terminate counselling prematurely. This may be due to a number of factors, some attributable to issues within your control and others attributable to issues outside your control.

Issues which are within your control that may have a negative impact on your clients include the following.

Lack of interest

Your clients will soon discern whether or not you are interested in them. Common signs of counsellor lack of interest include: making frequent requests for your clients to repeat themselves; yawning; getting basic information wrong about your client, such as their name, marital and family status; and confusing the client with other clients.

An environment not conducive to counselling

Have you ever consulted someone when your interaction with that person was frequently interrupted by outside sources? What impact did that have on you? My guess is that it was quite negative. For counselling to be effective it has to take place within an environment that is free from interruptions. If you take phone calls from others in a counselling session, or if you are interrupted by a receptionist, this will lead your clients to conclude that you are not interested in them. It is also crucial that noise from outside does not intrude into counselling sessions. Many years ago I was interviewed for a post of student counsellor. The counsellor was expected to see clients in a portakabin where conversations taking place next door could be clearly heard. At interview, when I mentioned at the outset that counselling could not properly proceed in such an environment, I was told that the accommodation could not be changed and that if I wanted to withdraw my application they would pay my travelling expenses! You cannot expect your clients to think that you have their interests at heart if you cannot provide them with an environment that is free from interruption and intrusion. Privacy is crucial to counselling, and if you cannot provide it then your attempts to facilitate your client's exploration will either not get under way or will falter quickly if they do.

Poor basic counselling skills

Virtually all counselling courses that have as their aim preparing trainees to practise begin by training them in basic counselling skills (or have applicants demonstrate that they have had such basic training before being accepted on to the course). However, just because someone has received training in basic counselling skills does not mean that they can demonstrate them routinely in practice. Therefore, if you fail to listen to your clients, fail to show that you understand them or fail to encourage them to talk in their own way, then you will not succeed in engaging them in a productive process of self-exploration.

Being judgemental

When you demonstrate a negatively judgemental attitude to what your clients are saying, then these clients will in all probability feel reluctant to open up to you. Showing disapproval of the things that clients say demonstrates to them, rightly or wrongly, that you disapprove of them as people. If clients sense this, then they will soon leave counselling or be very selective in what they are prepared to discuss. As such their exploration will be highly curtailed.

Does the counsellor have sufficient expertise to help me?

I mentioned in Chapter 2 that some clients are more concerned with your expertise as a counsellor than whether or not they like you or feel comfortable talking to you. Such clients will tend to disclose themselves more fully if they see you as knowledgeable and expert. While it is important that you do not claim knowledge and expertise you do not have, it is perfectly legitimate for you to capitalise with such clients on the knowledge and expertise that you do have. You can do this is a number of ways.

Emphasise your qualifications

If you have finished your counsellor training, then why not put your diploma on prominent display? After all, you have earned it and some of your clients will be impressed by seeing it; similarly for any accreditation certificates that you may possess. However, if you are still in training it is important that you make this clear at the outset. It is unethical not to do so. However, since my trainees tell me that their clients seem to think that 'counsellor in training' sounds more professional than 'trainee counsellor', you may wish to use that term with those of your clients who are concerned with matters of knowledge and expertise.

Make your consulting room look as professional as possible

Putting your certificates on the wall is only one way of making your room look professional. Making sure that your bookshelves are amply stocked with books on counselling is another. It is also important to remove items that might otherwise detract from the professional atmosphere of your consulting room.

Quote the research literature

In my view it is very important that you keep abreast of developments in research on counselling. You should do this primarily to be a more effective practitioner, but if it helps some clients to explore themselves more fully, then why not quote them relevant research findings when it is appropriate to do so.

Write and suggest that your clients read your writings, if relevant

If you have written anything that is relevant to the problems of those of your clients who will be positively influenced by your expertise, then suggest that they read it. They are likely to be impressed with the fact that you have written something and may explore themselves more fully as a result.

Cognitive-experiential understanding

The three major approaches discussed in this book and represented in this series (psychodynamic, person-centred and CBT) all consider that a major purpose of self-exploration is to foster a new understanding of self, others and the world, particularly – but not exclusively – with respect to the problems for which they originally sought counselling.

The three approaches all argue that cognitive understanding alone is insufficient to promote meaningful change, In order for change to be meaningful, understanding has to have both cognitive and emotional-experiential components. In this respect, Howard (2010: 3) quotes Cozolino (2002) who, she says, 'proposes that the simultaneous firing of previously dissociated neural circuits associated with feeling and understanding leads to psychological integration as they come together'.

Where the three approaches differ concerns the constituents of such feeling-based understanding. Thus, in psychodynamic counselling what is important is for clients to gain an emotionally based understanding of the connection between past and present ways of behaving, including the ways in which the clients interact with their counsellors. In person-centred counselling, what is important is for clients to engage in a deepening process of self-exploration initiated earlier in the process, while in CBT the clients work with their counsellors to develop a case formulation where they understand how their beliefs, emotions and behaviours are connected to explain the maintenance of their problems. These two latter approaches differ from psychodynamic counselling in that they advocate going back to the clients' past if taken there by the clients themselves, rather than as a matter of course, as tends to be the case in the psychodynamic approach. On the other hand, CBT (particularly REBT) sees that cognitive understanding in most cases precedes experiential understanding and that it is legitimate for the counsellor to promote the former before the latter. In this approach experiential understanding is promoted by the consistent application of cognitive, emotive and behavioural methods used in concert. Psychodynamic and person-centred counselling place far less emphasis on techniques and consider that a corrective emotional experience is more likely to occur in counselling sessions than between sessions, whereas CBT sees such experience as more likely to occur between sessions.

Working alliance theory holds that a number of things tend to take place in each of the four domains when progress towards cognitive-experiential understanding occurs at this stage. First, in the *bond* domain, clients develop greater trust in you, are more likely to withstand difficulties in the relationship than in the earlier stages, and benefit increasingly, where appropriate, from your expertise. Despite the rough patches that are common as your clients struggle to change painful patterns and at the same time to hold on to them because they provide familiarity and predictability, you and your clients have become used to one another and have settled down into a productive working relationship.

This productive relationship in the *task* domain is characterised by clients developing a greater understanding of what they have to do in counselling and what you are doing and by clients engaging more deeply in their tasks. For you, as counsellor, perhaps the greatest task is the timing of interventions. Going too slowly insufficiently stretches clients and the impetus of change is lost. Going too fast too soon tends to engender resistance in clients because they are being asked to change too quickly and too little appreciation is taken of their defences. As Anna Freud (1946) showed many years ago, clients erect a number of psychological defences against change and skilful counsellors across the approaches take clients' defences very much into account when intervening in the *task* domain.

In the *views* domain, you and your clients share a more sophisticated understanding of the latter's difficulties and the relevant determinants of these difficulties. As the name of this stage makes clear, such understanding is experientially as well as cognitively understood by clients, setting the stage for later changes to be made on the basis of this felt understanding.

Finally, in the *goals* domain of the alliance, you and your clients refine the latter's goals according to a more sophisticated understanding of the clients' problems generated in this stage. Sometimes clients' goals do not alter throughout counselling, but sometimes they change considerably. Counsellors who succeed in engaging their clients in what I have called the 'reflection process' (see p. 84) and encourage clients to understand that their goals may well change as counselling proceeds, tend to be far more helpful to their clients than counsellors who work on the assumption that, once negotiated at the outset, clients' goals do not alter.

In addition, at this stage when the work is going well, clients become increasingly sure about the relationship between what you and they are doing in the *task* domain and where they are heading in the *goals* domain.

Change based on cognitive-experiential understanding

Once clients have achieved a measure of cognitive-experiential understanding they need to capitalise on this and make changes. Such changes can be behavioural and/or philosophical in nature.

Behavioural change based on cognitive-experiential understanding

While stage-based models of the counselling process are meant to highlight broad differences of emphasis at each stage, it should not be thought that there is no overlap between what goes on between stages. This is particularly the case in considering the difference between the previous stage ('cognitive-experiential understanding') and this one, which focuses more on action taken on the basis of such understanding. For example, remember the point that I made in the previous section about REBT's view of the difference between cognitive and experiential understanding. In this approach one of the best ways in which experiential understanding can be fostered is through action based on and consistent with cognitive understanding.

Having made this point, it is the case in the major approaches to counselling that unless clients act on their new cognitive and experientially felt insights, meaningful and enduring change is unlikely to occur. These approaches do differ in how they deal with the issue of client action. In CBT, it is dealt with explicitly and directly and clients are encouraged to carry out properly negotiated behavioural assignments between sessions. When most successful, these assignments reflect the new understanding that clients have derived from the earlier stages and are based on a clear and shared view of how these assignments will help clients move closer to their goals. Emphasising the importance of these assignments is a core counsellor task in CBT and is done by devoting sufficient time to the process of homework negotiation and to the review of such assignments in the subsequent session. To reflect the importance of such assignments in the counselling process, my colleague, Ray DiGiuseppe (personal communication), urges REBT therapists to view the structure of counselling sessions as follows: (1) review homework assignments; (2) do session work; (3) negotiate homework assignments.

In both psychodynamic and person-centred counselling there is far less *routine* structured emphasis on encouraging clients to act on their new cognitive-experiential understanding. Having said that, person-centred counsellors will work with specific behavioural home-work assignments if the wish to do so is suggested by clients and emerges from the preceding work. Person-centred counsellors tend to shy away from suggesting the use of such assignments since they are loath to impose their frame of reference on their clients. However, if person-centred counsellors experience a strong and persistent felt sense that the use of such assignments would be helpful to their clients then they are encouraged to voice this felt sense, but to own it as their own feeling and not to impose it on their clients. However, if in response their clients do wish to make use of such assignments, then their counsellors will proceed on this basis. In person-centred counsel-ling, here as elsewhere, the preservation of client autonomy is a guiding principle as it should ethically be in all approaches to counselling (BACP, 2010).

Leaving aside the use of structured behavioural homework assign-ments, both psychodynamic and person-centred counsellors tend to share the view that action will naturally follow the acquisition of cognitive-experiential understanding. When such action does not ensue then either the person's understanding is cognitive in nature and lacks the experiential base, or the client is experiencing some other block to action. In psychodynamic counselling this 'resistance' to change is located and interpreted in terms of the counsellor's own view of the client's conflicts or deficits (Howard, 2010), while in person-centred counselling the 'block' is explored until the 'resistance' is experienced, accepted and thus loses its power to impede action.

In CBT, part of the emphasis at this stage is in teaching clients new behavioural skills. Such skills include social skills for people who are shy and have not developed basic skills such as maintaining eye contact; presentation skills for those who are nervous about public speaking; and test-taking skills for those who are anxious in examination settings.

Person-centred counsellors tend not to teach their clients new skills as an integral part of this approach, but may do so if the wish emanates from the clients themselves or if the felt sense to do so is strong and persistent and shared with the client. For this to become the focus of person-centred counselling, the client needs to voice agreement to focus on developing new behavioural skills before both client and counsellor do so. Psychodynamic counsellors tend not to teach their clients new skills even if asked to do so by the clients themselves. Over the years, as a CBT counsellor I have had many self-referrals from people who have got a lot from psychodynamic counsellors but have ended up becoming frustrated by their counsellors' refusal to teach them new skills when persistently asked to do so by the clients. 'I don't work in this way' is the counsellors' response most often reported by clients who leave psychodynamic counselling for CBT. By stating this, my intention is not to trumpet CBT's superiority over psychodynamic counselling (I am sure that over the years some of my clients have sought psychodynamic counselling, having become frustrated with REBT), but to emphasise what can happen when an approach to counselling fails to meet client need at this stage of counselling.

As I mentioned above, it often happens that when clients act on their new cognitive-experiential understanding they tend to deepen this understanding. Thus, the work done at this stage often reinforces the gains made in the previous stage. All approaches to counselling recognise this important point.

Philosophical change based on cognitive-experiential understanding

It sometimes happens that acting differently is not relevant to clients' problems. Thus clients' emotional problems may concern past behaviour (for example, guilt or shame), or it may be the case that acting differently is not going to change the adversities that the clients are facing (for example, an incurable illness). As the famous serenity prayer advises: 'God grant me the serenity to accept the things I cannot change; courage to change the things I can; and wisdom to know the difference.' At this stage of counselling, you need to help your clients develop (a) the wisdom to know that they need to make what I call here philosophical change (by which I mean a fundamental change in outlook) without reference to behavioural change; and (b) the serenity to do this. The major approaches will do this in different ways. The biggest difference here will be between CBT and the other two approaches. For example, in REBT we may well teach clients about the concepts of acceptance and self-acceptance and show them specifically how to do accept themselves for their past behaviour (Dryden, 2003), and to accept grim reality when they cannot change what they may wish to change.

In person-centred counselling, the view is that as the relationship deepens between counsellor and client, the latter will engage in deeper self-exploration and express the profound pain of what they have done in the past, or the unchanging adversities of the present. Engaging in such deep processes facilitates self-acceptance and/or acceptance of what cannot be changed. However, it is the experiencing of unconditional acceptance from the counsellor that particularly enables the client to begin this process of self-acceptance which will enable change to take place. In addition, Casemore (2011) suggests that the client's experiencing of acceptance by the counsellor provides the platform for stronger and sustained challenge from the therapist which again facilitates change.

In psychodynamic counselling the emphasis is more on helping clients gain deeper understanding of the intra-psychic meaning of their past behaviour or of the present unchanging adversity, to relate this to their conflicts and to interpret blocks to self- and life-acceptance. Finally, I want to make the point that while I have considered behavioural change and philosophical change separately, in reality they can occur together.

Working through

Once clients have acted on their new cognitive-experiential understanding and/or developed a new constructive outlook on the adversities in their life that cannot be changed, then they need to be helped to capitalise on their gains and be prepared to deal with lapses so they can avoid total relapse.

Helping clients to capitalise on their gains

In my experience as a counsellor, most clients do not naturally generalise what they learn in counselling from one area of their lives to others. For example, I once helped a client to deal with her need for her boss's approval to the extent that she asserted herself constructively with her boss. A few sessions later, she came in with a very similar issue – non-assertion for fear of incurring her friend's disapproval. Before exploring this issue with her, I found that while she could see the similarity between her need for her friend's approval and her need for her boss's approval when it was pointed out to her, she had not been able to see it for herself before the connection was put to her. In addition, she said that she did not think of generalising what she had learned about dealing with her boss's disapproval to dealing with her friend's disapproval.

This shows that most clients need help to generalise their gains from one area to related areas and this is a major counsellor task in the working-through process. CBT counsellors actively address this task and will use the cognitive-behavioural conceptualisation that they developed with their clients earlier in the counselling process, and modified as counselling proceeded, as a structured way of doing this. Psychodynamic counsellors will do this by using interventions that connect and interpret (for example, 'Can you see the relationship between needing the approval of your father and needing the approval of the male authority figures in your life?'), while person-centred counsellors would share these connections tentatively at first, whenever they experience the strong felt sense to do so, taking care not to take the exploration away from the frame of reference of their clients.

Working with and anticipating lapses to prevent relapse

It is accepted by counsellors from all the major counselling approaches, that once clients make progress in counselling, they may experience lapses in their progress. A lapse is different from a relapse in the following respect. While a lapse is a significant, but temporary, falling back along the road to recovery, a relapse is a more fundamental and enduring return to the original problem state which prompted help-seeking in the first place. The two most important things at this stage of the coun-selling process are (1) to help your clients learn from their lapses so that they don't become relapses; and (2) to help them anticipate lapses so that they can learn to deal with the relevant factors before they lapse. It is important to help clients identify what may be called their vulner-ability factors, that is, factors to which they are particularly vulnerable.

CBT counsellors tend to do this 'lapse work' in a structured but col-laborative way, using tasks with which their clients are likely to be familiar to help them identify and deal effectively with the situational, cognitive, emotive, behavioural and interpersonal factors that under-pin the clients' tendencies to lapse. Thus, written diaries are employed for identification purposes, and cognitive, behavioural and imagery techniques are used for intervention purposes. As before, psychody-namic counsellors tend to help their clients identify the factors involved in a less structured way and will not suggest specific tech-niques that clients can use to deal with lapses. Rather, they will clarify the relevant issues and then use interpretation to help their clients understand the idiosyncratic reasons for their lapsing. Person-centred counsellors deal with this issue as they deal with other issues. They convey respect for clients even though they have lapsed and strive to convey their understanding of their clients' experience before, dur-ing and after lapsing. In this way their clients can look without shame or anxiety at what their experience was, so that they can learn from it. Any specific techniques employed during this process are used with mutual consent, but the first suggestion to do so normally emanates from the clients themselves.

Handing over the reins to the client

A final counsellor task during the working-through process involves helping clients to become their own counsellors. When counselling is at its most effective, clients not only achieve their goals but take away from the process a way of helping themselves in the future, one which is influenced by the counselling approach practised by their counsellors. Thus, clients in psychodynamic counselling whose problems are rooted in conflict learn to identify the conflicts that underpin their urges to act in dysfunctional ways, and to interpret the conflicts for themselves so that they can respond to the situations they face in the present, uncontaminated by past conflicts. Clients in person-centred counselling learn to show themselves empathy, warmth and respect so they can be honest with themselves and respect their experiences, without trying to fit these experiences into false and often idealised self-structures.

Clients in CBT take away from this form of counselling (1) a specific framework by which to identify and analyse their experiences, and (2) a range of specific techniques to employ when necessary. The major difference between these three approaches is that while clients in effective psychodynamic and person-centred counselling learn by internalising their respective ways of approaching these problems, clients in CBT learn by being taught how to use these tasks by their counsellors. There is little, if any, such formal teaching in the two other approaches.

Ending

The ending of counselling relationships is often deemed to be a difficult time for clients, echoing their difficulties in saying goodbye and in dealing with loss. This view tends to be held mainly by psychodynamic and person-centred counsellors. The reason for this is twofold. First, since they do not aim to teach clients how to use a specific framework and a variety of techniques, the focus is more on the relationship as a vehicle for change (the 'I–thou' relationship that develops in person-centred counselling and the 'as-if' relationship that develops in psychodynamic counselling). Secondly, while all three approaches can be short- and long-term, psychodynamic and person-centred counselling tend to be longer-term than CBT. These two factors may explain the greater importance accorded to ending counselling and its vicissitudes in psychodynamic and person-centred counselling than in CBT. In the latter, no assumption is made that ending is bound to be difficult for clients, although due recognition is given to the idea that it can be so for a proportion of clients.

When ending counselling is deemed to be difficult for clients then it is very important that you give due time to helping these clients deal with and work through their feelings about the ending of the counselling relationship, whichever approach you practise. This is particularly the case when the end of the counselling relationship is definite. I say this because it is increasingly the case that counselling tends to fade out rather than end definitively, because ever-increasing gaps occur between sessions. This has the effect of diluting the importance of counselling's end. Psychodynamic counsellors, in particular, lament this practice because such dilution prevents clients from facing up to and working through their feelings about the painful reality of loss of important relationships.

A note on dealing with 'obstacles to change'

Throughout this book I have attempted to show how working alliance theory can shed light on the process of counselling. I have made it clear which factors tend to enhance counselling and which factors tend to impede it. In this final chapter, it should be clear that there are many obstacles to progress in counselling and these can exist at all the stages of counselling I have discussed in this chapter. Indeed, a thorough discussion of such obstacles and how to deal with them warrants a very large volume. What I do want to emphasise here is that the best way to deal with obstacles is to follow a simple set of steps.

1 Identify the obstacles.
2 Encourage your clients to give their view of the obstacles.
3 Show clients full respect. Do not denigrate your clients in any way.

4 Show empathy with your clients concerning the difficulty of change.
5 Encourage your clients to stand back and reflect on the factors that contribute to the obstacles, and that need to be changed.
6 If you are the obstacle, acknowledge this non-defensively and undertake to change what you have been doing. Apologise to your clients if necessary.
7 If the obstacles are not attributable to you, help your clients to brainstorm ways of dealing with the factors that have contributed to the obstacles.
8 Help your clients evaluate possible ways of dealing with these factors and encourage them to select the ones that seem most likely to be effective.
9 Evaluate the clients' attempts to implement the above procedures.
10 Continue with steps 7, 8 and 9 until the clients have dealt with the obstacles to change.

If you want to read about how to deal with threats to the working alliance across the counselling process, I recommend Safran and Muran (2000).

Discussion issues

1 How do your views on the process of counselling differ from mine?
2 In your view, what are the most common obstacles to client change in the counselling process and how do you address them?
3 How do you approach the issue of dealing with client lapses and relapse prevention?
4 What do you think of the idea of encouraging your clients to become their own counsellors in the ending phase of the counselling process?
5 How do you help clients prepare for the end of counselling?

A final note

My aim in writing this book was to take a general view of counselling in a nutshell and one that is not specifically aligned with any specific approach to counselling. I have tried to be fair-minded, but since I am influenced most by CBT in my work, I recognise that this bias is present. I do not apologise for this. Counselling is a personal process and thus if I withheld my personal views completely it would have the effect of depersonalising the book. Therefore, as you read and hopefully re-read this book, I would encourage you to identify my personal biases, engage with them, reflect on them and if by doing so they encourage you to be clearer about your own views of counselling in a nutshell, then one of the goals that I had in writing this book would have been achieved.

Appendix 1[1]

AMY HELPER
11 Anywhere House, Anywhere Street, London SE7 OET
Tel: 020 8852 5453. Fax: 020 8852 2071.
Email: amy@internet.com Website: www.amyhelper.com

Client information sheet

Training

MSc in Counselling, Diploma in Cognitive-Behavioural Counselling.

Accreditation

BACP Senior Registered Practitioner and BABCP Accredited Cognitive-Behavioural Psychotherapist.

Experience

I have experience of working in a variety of private, local authority, voluntary, public and medical sectors.

Codes of ethics

---

[1] In this appendix, I present one counsellor's way of providing clients with information about the approach to counselling being offered, the practicalities of counselling, the limits to absolute confidentiality and other relevant information.

I abide by the British Association for Counselling and Psychotherapy (BACP) and British Association for Behavioural and Cognitive Psychotherapies (BABCP) codes of ethics.

Fees

Payment by an individual (cash or cheque) is made at the end of each session. Organisations are invoiced on a monthly basis or at the end of a given contract period. Fees are subject to VAT and annual review and non-payment of fees may result in legal action being taken.

Individuals	£50.00
Couples	£70.00

Cancellation policy

A full **24 hours' notice** is required for cancelled appointments otherwise the full fee is payable.

Supervision

Good practice requires regular supervision of cases as this ensures that standards are maintained in both counselling and coaching.

Confidentiality and access to case notes

The trust between client and practitioner is crucial to the success of the process and we treat all information disclosed as confidential. Any details a supervisor receives are also treated as confidential and I do not disclose client details to a third party without the client's permission. However, if in my opinion a client is a danger to him/herself or to others

I reserve the right to inform appropriate agencies. It is my practice, wherever possible, to inform the client first. I keep brief notes following each session that you are entitled to see if you so wish.

Process

All prospective clients are offered an Assessment Interview. This provides both parties with an opportunity to consider whether they wish to work together. It is just as important that you feel comfortable with your therapist, as it is that he or she feels able to work with you. At the end of the first session we would arrange to meet for an agreed number of sessions.

There is no obligation to attend all the sessions arranged and you are free to terminate your appointments at any time. A review session takes place at the end of the agreed number of sessions where we jointly assess progress and what further action, if any, may be needed. If we decide not to work together we try to provide you with details of alternative practitioners or agencies.

Sessions usually last for one hour and if you are late arriving we still terminate at the usual time so as not to delay the next person. I leave 15 minutes between sessions to allow those people wishing to remain anonymous the opportunity of doing so. I see clients during the day as well as in the evening, and special appointments can be arranged for the weekend.

Contact

There are times when I may not be available for various reasons. To allow messages to get through I have a confidential voicemail service that we encourage clients to use. If I need to make contact with you we simply leave our name and telephone number should you be unavailable.

How can therapy help me?

A therapist is someone who will help you move forward with your life, helping you in practical ways to design an action plan that will give you the greatest chance of reaching your goal. In addition a therapist aims to help you gain a perspective about whatever is troubling you. Together we identify what might be stopping you from reaching your full potential and what action you need to take to change your situation.

Therapists look beyond presenting problems to possible underlying causes. The aim of therapy is to help you change your behaviour to that which is more productive for you. The process helps you move towards becoming the kind of person you want to be by attaining the types of outcomes you desire both personally and professionally.

My approach

There are many different models of coaching and counselling to choose from. I do not believe there is one model that helps everyone, as each person is an individual and what might suit one person may not necessarily suit another. However, I believe in using interactive forms of intervention as reflected in the training of Associates. I aim to be sensitive to the cultural and ethnic origins of individuals and to people's religious beliefs and sexual orientation. I operate our practice along the lines normally associated with an equal opportunities employer.

How to find me

By Train: Just 12 minutes from Central London. Trains leave Charing Cross, Victoria, Waterloo East and London Bridge towards Bexleyheath/Dartford – usually at least four trains an hour. Our offices are about a 10–15 minute walk from Blackheath Station. There is a minicab company at the side of the station and the cost is approximately £3.00.

By car: The A2, A20 and South Circular Road for quick and easy access.

By bus: Numbers 54, 89, 108, 202, N53 and N108 all stop in Anywhere Street.

Parking: There are parking bays available in Streetfield Mews.

Issues for you to consider

Here is a list of topics or questions you may wish to raise when attending your initial interview:

a   Check your practitioner has the relevant qualifications and experience.
b   Check the approach the practitioner uses, and how it relates to your problem.
c   Check that the practitioner is in Supervision (a professional requirement).
d   Check that the practitioner is a member of a professional body and abides by a code of ethics.
e   Discuss your expectations of Life Coaching, Counselling or Psychotherapy and the goals you want to achieve.
f   Ask about fees and discuss the frequency and estimated duration of sessions.
g   Arrange regular review sessions with your practitioner to evaluate your progress.
h   Do not be coerced into a long-term contract unless you are satisfied that it is necessary and beneficial to you.

If you do not have a chance to discuss the above points during your first session, discuss them at the next possible opportunity.

General issues

1   Practitioner self-disclosure can be useful. However, if sessions are dominated by the practitioner discussing his/her own problems at length, raise this in the session.
2   If you feel uncomfortable, undermined or manipulated at any time within the session, discuss this with the practitioner. It is easier to resolve issues as and when they arise.

3   It is unethical for a practitioner to engage in sexual activity with current clients and research has shown it is not beneficial for clients to have sexual contact with their practitioner.

4   Do not accept gifts from your practitioner. This does not apply to relevant therapeutic material.

5   Do not accept social invitations from your practitioner. However, this does not apply to relevant assignments such as being accompanied into a situation to help you overcome a phobia.

6   If your practitioner proposes a change in venue without good reason (e.g. from a centre to the person's home) do not agree.

7   If you have any doubts about the treatment you are receiving, discuss them with your practitioner. If you are still uncertain, seek advice and/or terminate your work.

8   You have the right to terminate your work at any time you wish.

(Adapted from Palmer and Szymanska, 1994.)

References

Adler, A. (1979) *Superiority and Social Interest* (3rd rev. edn). New York: Norton.

Barker, C., Pistrang, N., Shapiro, D.A. and Shaw, I. (1990) 'Coping and help-seeking in the UK adult population', *British Journal of Clinical Psychology*, 29: 271–85.

Beck, A.T., Rush, A.J., Shaw, B.F. and Emery, G. (1979) *Cognitive Therapy of Depression*. New York: Guilford.

Beitman, B.D. (1987) *The Structure of Individual Psychotherapy*. New York: Guilford.

Beutler, L.E. and Harwood, T.M. (2000) *Prescriptive Psychotherapy: A Practical Guide to Systematic Treatment Selection*. New York: Oxford University Press.

Beutler, L.E., Crago, M. and Arizmendi, T.G. (1986) 'Therapist variables in psychotherapy process and outcome', in S.L. Garfield and A.E. Bergin (eds), *Handbook of Psychotherapy and Behavior Change* (3rd edition). New York: John Wiley & Sons, Inc.

Beutler, L.E., Malik, M., Alimohammed, S., Harwood, T.M., Talebi, H., Noble, S. and Wong, E. (2004) 'Therapist variables', in M.J. Lambert, *Bergin and Garfield's Handbook of Psychotherapy and Behavior Change* (5th edition). New York: John Wiley & Sons, Inc.

Bond, T. (2000) *Standards and Ethics for Counselling in Action* (2nd edition). London: Sage.

Bordin, E.S. (1979) 'The generalizability of the psychoanalytic concept of the working alliance', *Psychotherapy: Theory, Research and Practice*, 16 (3): 252–60.

British Association for Counselling and Psychotherapy (2010) *Ethical Framework for Good Practice in Counselling and Psychotherapy* (Revised edition). Lutterworth, Leicestershire: BACP.

Casemore, R. (2006) *Person-centred Counselling in a Nutshell*. London: Sage.

Casemore, R. (2011) *Person-centred Counselling in a Nutshell* (2nd edition). London: Sage.

Cozolino, L. (2002) *The Neuroscience of Psychotherapy: Building and Rebuilding the Human Brain.* New York: Norton.

Dorn, F.J. (ed.) (1984) *The Social Influence Process in Counseling and Psychotherapy.* Springfield, IL: Charles C. Thomas.

Dryden, W. (1985) 'Challenging, but not overwhelming: a compromise in negotiating homework assignments', *British Journal of Cognitive Psychotherapy*, 3(1): 77–80.

Dryden, W. (2003) *Managing Low Self-esteem.* London: Whurr.

Dryden, W. (2004) *Rational Emotive Behaviour Therapy Clients' Manual.* London: Whurr.

Dryden, W. and Reeves, A. (eds) (2008) *Key Issues for Counselling in Action* (2nd edition). London: Sage.

Egan, G. (2002) *The Skilled Helper: A Problem-management and Opportunity-development Approach to Helping* (7th edition). Belmont, CA: Wadsworth.

Fong, M.L. and Gresback Cox, B. (1983) 'Trust as an underlying dynamic in the counseling process', *Personnel and Guidance Journal*, 62: 163–6.

Freud, A. (1946) *The Ego and the Mechanisms of Defense* (American edition). New York: International Universities Press.

Garvin, C.D. and Seabury, B.A. (1997) *Interpersonal Practice in Social Work: Promoting Competence and Social Justice* (2nd edition). Boston, MA: Allyn & Bacon.

Greenberg, L.S. (2002) *Emotion-focused Therapy: Coaching Clients to Work Through Their Feelings.* Washington, DC: American Psychological Association.

Howard, S. (2006) *Psychodynamic Counselling in a Nutshell.* London: Sage.

Howard, S. (2010) *Skills in Psychodynamic Counselling and Psychotherapy.* London: Sage.

Hutchins, D.E. (1984) 'Improving the counseling relationship', *Personnel and Guidance Journal*, 62: 572–5.

Klerman, G.L., Weissman, M.M., Rounsaville, B.J. and Chevron, E.S. (1984) *Interpersonal Psychotherapy of Depression*. New York: Basic Books.

Lambert, M.J. and Ogler, B.M. (2004) 'The efficacy and effectiveness of psychotherapy', in M.J. Lambert (ed.), *Bergin and Garfield's Handbook of Psychotherapy and Behavior Change* (5th edition). New York: John Wiley & Sons, Inc.

Lazarus, A. (ed.) (1985) *Casebook of Multimodal Therapy*. New York: Guilford.

Lazarus, A. (1989) *The Practice of Multimodal Therapy*. Baltimore, MD: Johns Hopkins University Press.

Lee, H. (1960) *To Kill a Mockingbird*. Philadelphia, PA: J.B. Lippincott.

Lemma, A. (2003) *Introduction to the Practice of Psychoanalytic Psychotherapy*. Chichester: John Wiley & Sons, Ltd.

Luborsky, L., McLellan, A.T., Woody, G.E., O'Brien, C.P. and Auerbach, A. (1985) 'Therapist success and its determinants', *Archives of General Psychiatry*, 42: 602–11.

McMahon, G. (2005) 'Coaching strategies: The boundaries between coaching and counselling', *Stress News*, 17(2), 17–18.

Mahrer, A. (ed.) (1967) *The Goals of Psychotherapy*. Englewood Cliffs, NJ: Prentice-Hall.

Maluccio, A.N. (1979) *Learning from Clients: Interpersonal Helping as Viewed by Clients and Social Workers*. New York: Free Press.

Mearns, D. and Cooper, M. (2005) *Working at Relational Depth in Counselling and Psychotherapy*. London: Sage.

Miller, W.R. and Rollnick, S. (2002) *Motivational Interviewing: Preparing People for Change* (2nd edition). New York: Guilford.

Orne, M.T. and Wender, P.H. (1968) 'Anticipatory socialization for psychotherapy: Methods and rationale', *American Journal of Psychiatry*, 124: 1202–12.

Palmer, S. and Szymanska, K. (1994) 'How to avoid being exploited in counselling and psychotherapy', *Counselling: Journal of the British Association for Counselling*, 5 (1): 24.

Pinsof, W.M. and Catherall, D. (1986) 'The integrative psychotherapy alliance: family, couple, individual therapy scales', *Journal of Marital and Family Therapy*, 12: 137–51.

Prochaska, J.O., Norcross, J.C. and DiClemente, C.C. (1994) *Changing for Good*. New York: William Morrow.

Rachman, S.J. and Wilson, G.T. (1980) *The Effects of Psychological Therapy* (2nd enlarged edition). New York: Pergamon.

Reeves, A. (2010) *Counselling Suicidal Clients*. London: Sage.

Rogers, C.R. (1957) 'The necessary and sufficient conditions of therapeutic personality change', *Journal of Consulting Psychology*, 21: 95–103.

Rogers, C.R. (1961) *On Becoming a Person: A Therapist's View of Psychotherapy*. London: Constable.

Safran, J.D. and Muran, J.C. (2000) *Negotiating the Therapeutic Alliance: A Relational Treatment Guide*. New York: Guilford.

Sanders, P. (2002) *First Steps in Counselling: A Students' Companion for Basic Introductory Courses*. Ross-on-Wye: PCCS Books.

Stiles, W.B., Shapiro, D.A. and Elliott, R. (1986) 'Are all psychotherapies equivalent?' *American Psychologist*, 41 (2): 165–80.

Woods, P. (1991) 'Orthodox RET taught effectively with graphics, feedback on irrational beliefs, a structured homework series and models of disputation', in M.E. Bernard (ed.), *Using Rational-emotive Therapy Effectively: A Practitioner's Guide*. New York: Plenum.

Index